The Land of No Hassles

CARTOONS BY John Heine

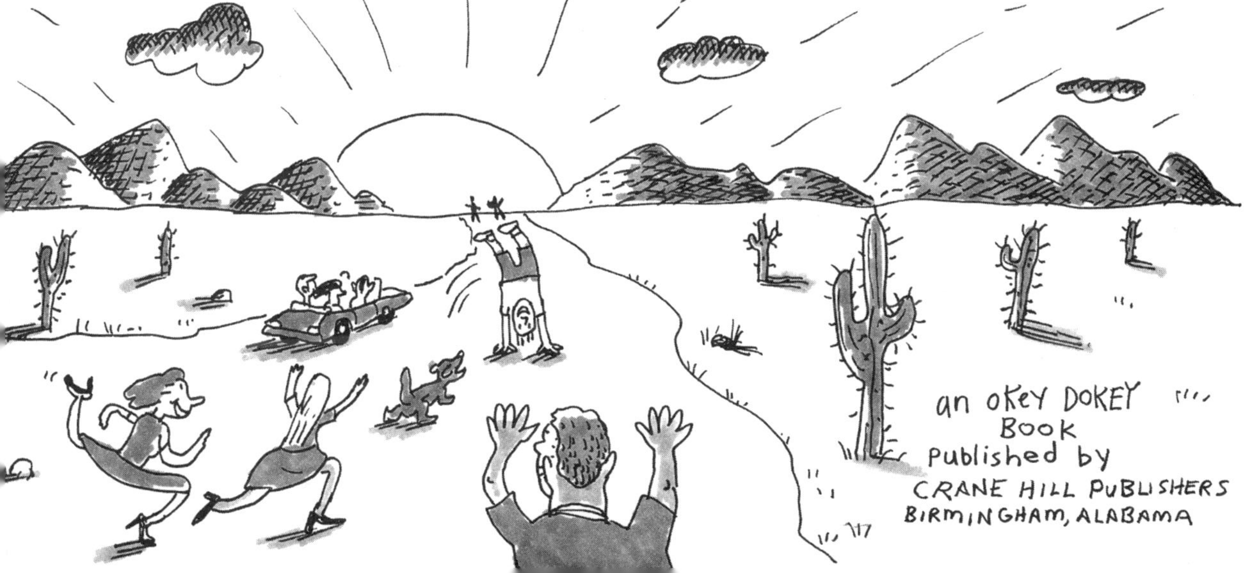

an OKEY DOKEY Book

published by
CRANE HILL PUBLISHERS
BIRMINGHAM, ALABAMA

Copyright © 1999 by John Heine

All rights reserved. With the exception of brief quotations in critical reviews or articles, no part of this work may be reproduced or transmitted in any form or by any means, electronic or mechanical, including photocopying, recording, or any information storage and retrieval system, without permission in writing from the publisher.

Published by Crane Hill Publishers, www.cranehill.com

Library of Congress Cataloging-ln-Publication Data

Heine. John. 1950-
The land of no hassles / by John Heine.
p.   cm.
ISBN 1-57587-107-6 (pbk.)
1. American wit and humor, Pictorial.   I. Title.
   NC1429.H377A4   1999
   741.5'973—dc2l   99-18883
                                                                                  CIP

10   9   8   7   6   5   4   3   2   1

<u>other books by John Heine</u>
A Good Planet is Hard To Find.
Southern Fried: True Views of the South.

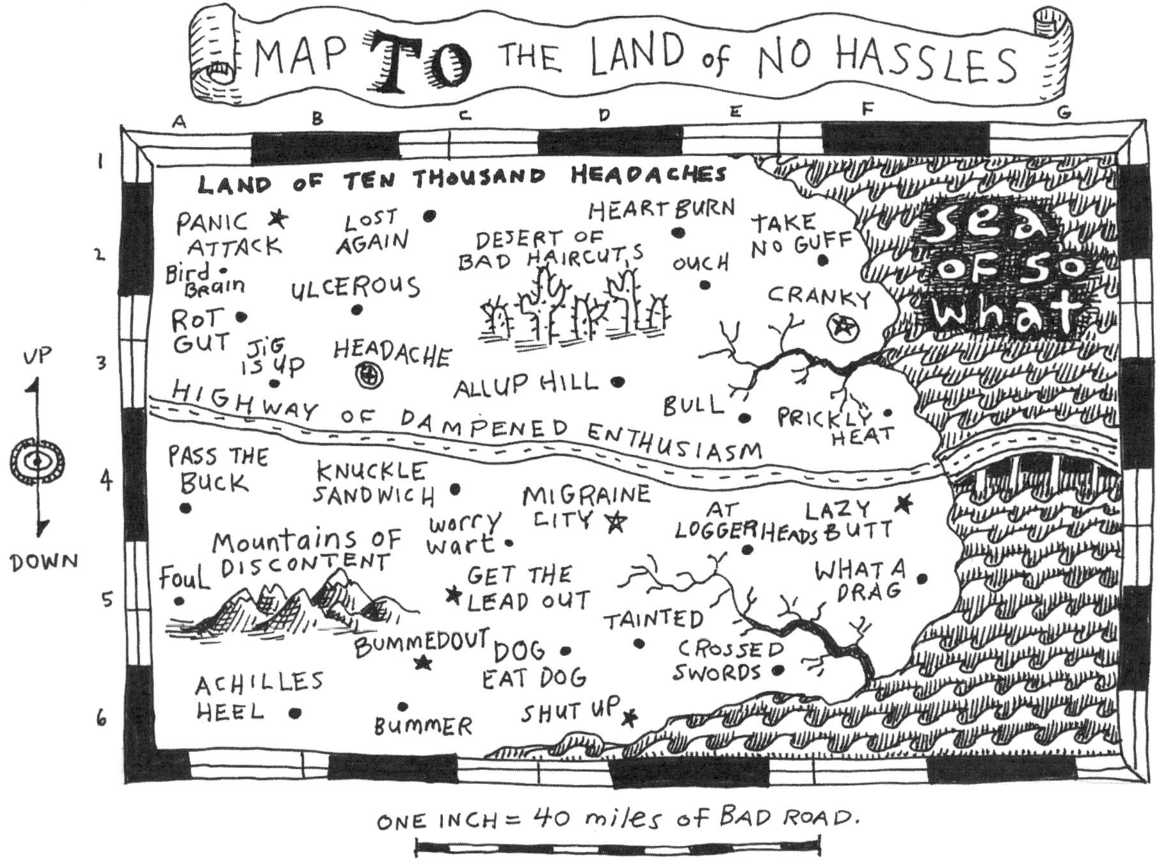
MAP TO THE LAND of NO HASSLES
A
B
C
D
E
F
G
1
2
3
4
5
6
UP
DOWN
LAND OF TEN THOUSAND HEADACHES
PANIC ATTACK
LOST AGAIN
HEART BURN
TAKE NO GUFF
DESERT OF BAD HAIRCUTS
Bird Brain
OUCH
ULCEROUS
CRANKY
Sea of So what
RoT GUT
JiG IS UP
HEADACHE
ALLUP HILL
BULL
PRICKLY HEAT
HIGHWAY OF DAMPENED ENTHUSIASM
PASS THE BUCK
KNUCKLE SANDWICH
MIGRAINE CITY
worry wart
AT LOGGERHEADS
LAZY BUTT
Mountains OF DISCONTENT
Foul
GET THE LEAD OUT
WHAT A DRAG
TAINTED
BUMMEDOUT
DOG EAT DOG
CROSSED SWORDS
ACHILLES HEEL
BUMMER
SHUT UP
ONE INCH = 40 miles of BAD ROAD.

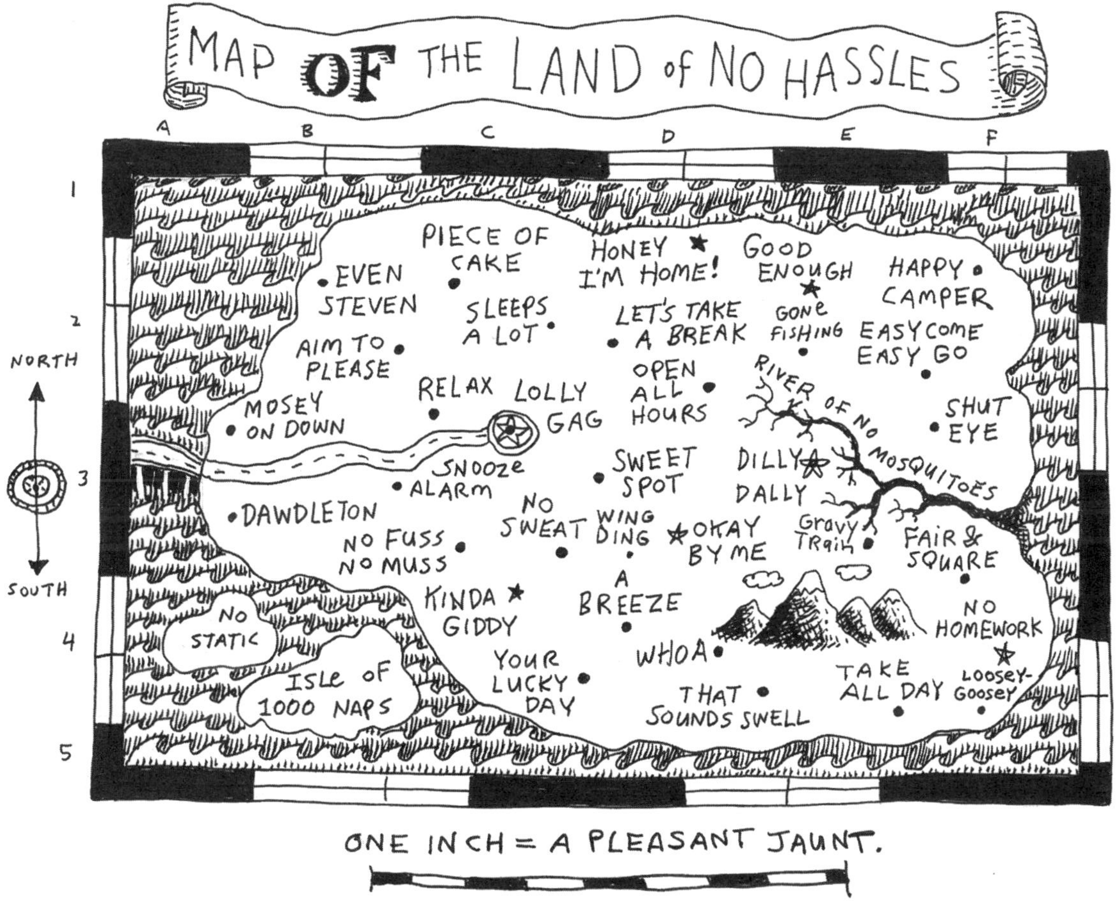
MAP OF THE LAND of NO HASSLES
A
B
C
D
E
F
1
2
3
4
5
NORTH
SOUTH
PIECE OF CAKE
HONEY I'M HOME!
GOOD ENOUGH
HAPPY CAMPER
EVEN STEVEN
SLEEPS A LOT
LET'S TAKE A BREAK
GONE FISHING
EASY COME EASY GO
AIM TO PLEASE
OPEN ALL HOURS
RIVER OF NO MOSQUITOES
RELAX
LOLLY GAG
MOSEY ON DOWN
SHUT EYE
SWEET SPOT
DILLY DALLY
SNOOZE ALARM
DAWDLETON
NO SWEAT
WING DING
OKAY BY ME
GRAVY TRAIN
FAIR & SQUARE
NO FUSS NO MUSS
KINDA GIDDY
A BREEZE
NO HOMEWORK
NO STATIC
ISLE OF 1000 NAPS
YOUR LUCKY DAY
WHOA
THAT SOUNDS SWELL
TAKE ALL DAY
LOOSEY-GOOSEY
ONE INCH = A PLEASANT JAUNT.

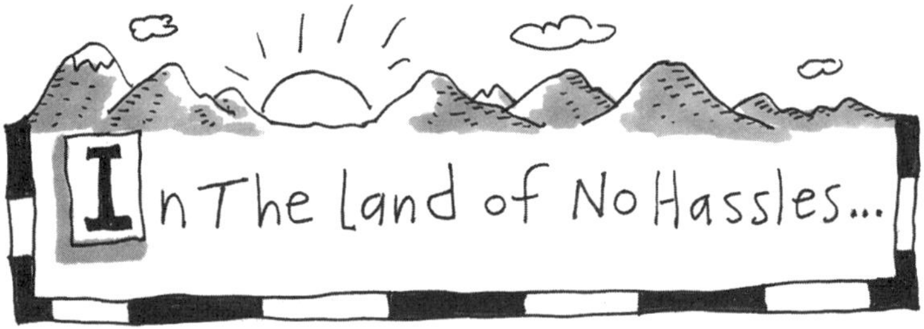
In The Land of No Hassles...

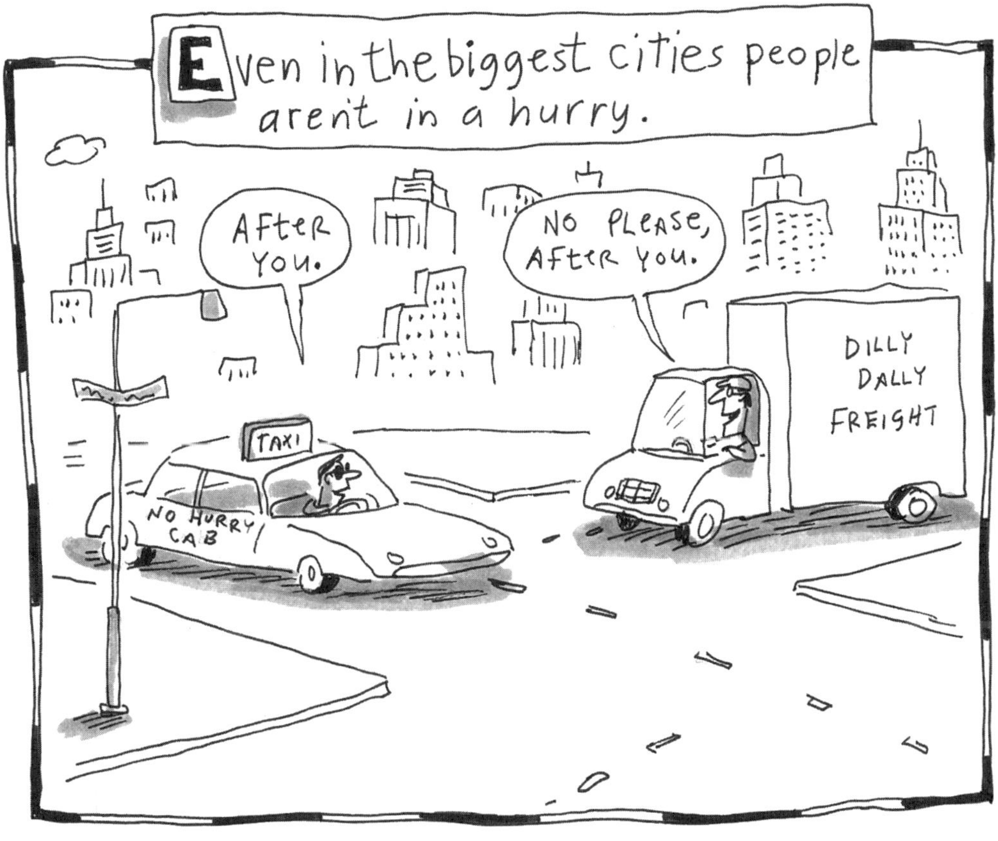
Even in the biggest cities people aren't in a hurry.
AFTER YOU.
NO PLEASE, AFTER YOU.
TAXI
NO HURRY CAB
DILLY DALLY FREIGHT

1

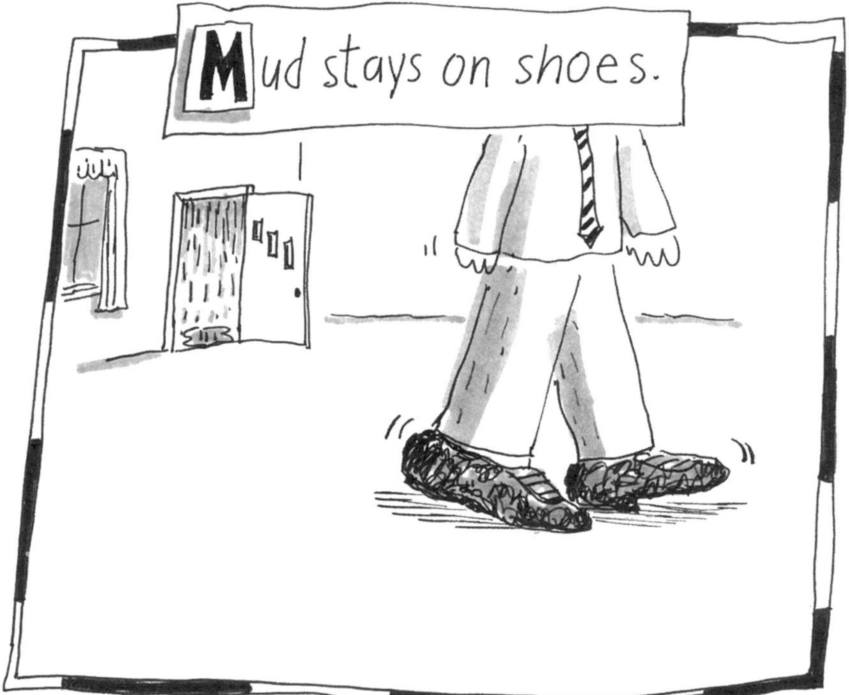
Mud stays on shoes.

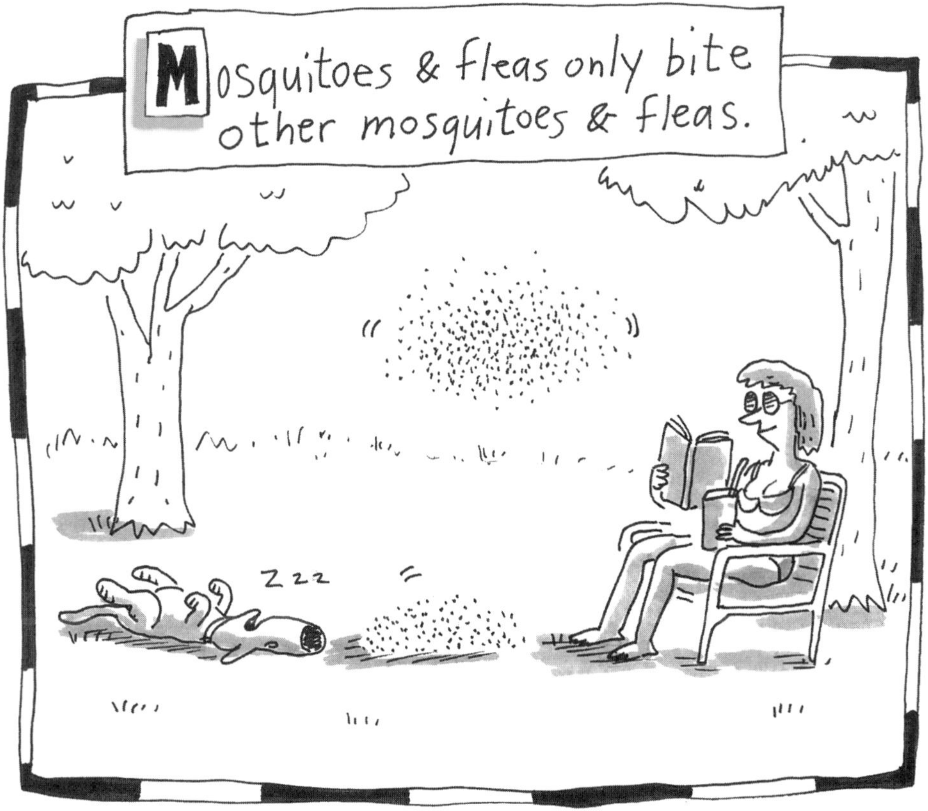
Mosquitoes & fleas only bite other mosquitoes & fleas.
Z z z

4

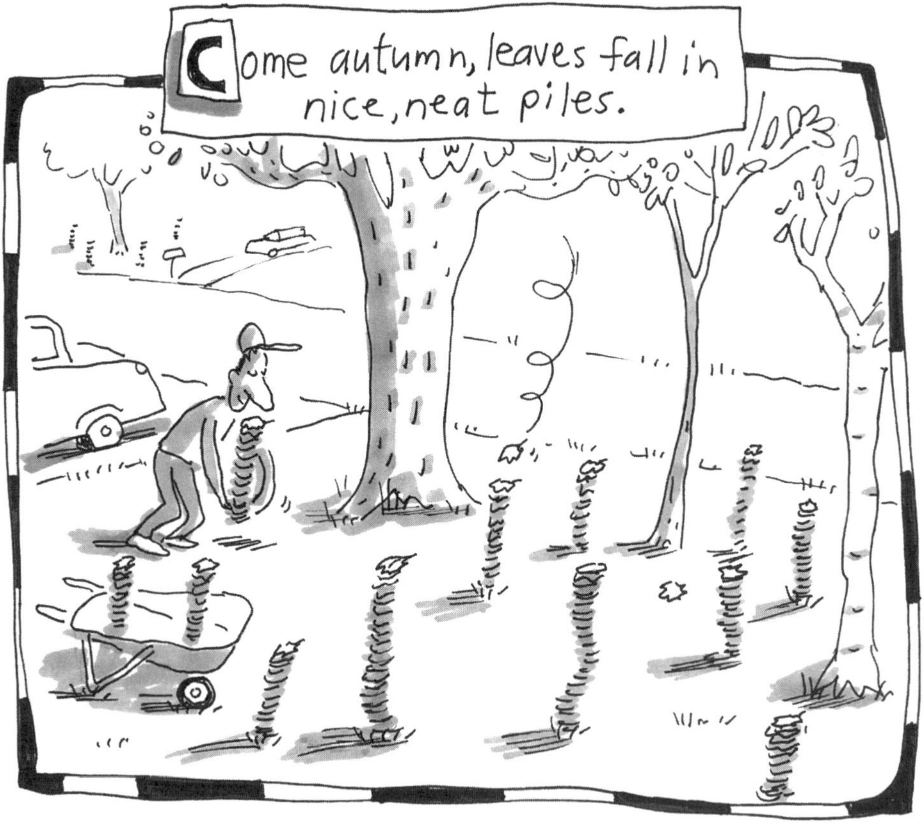
Come autumn, leaves fall in nice, neat piles.

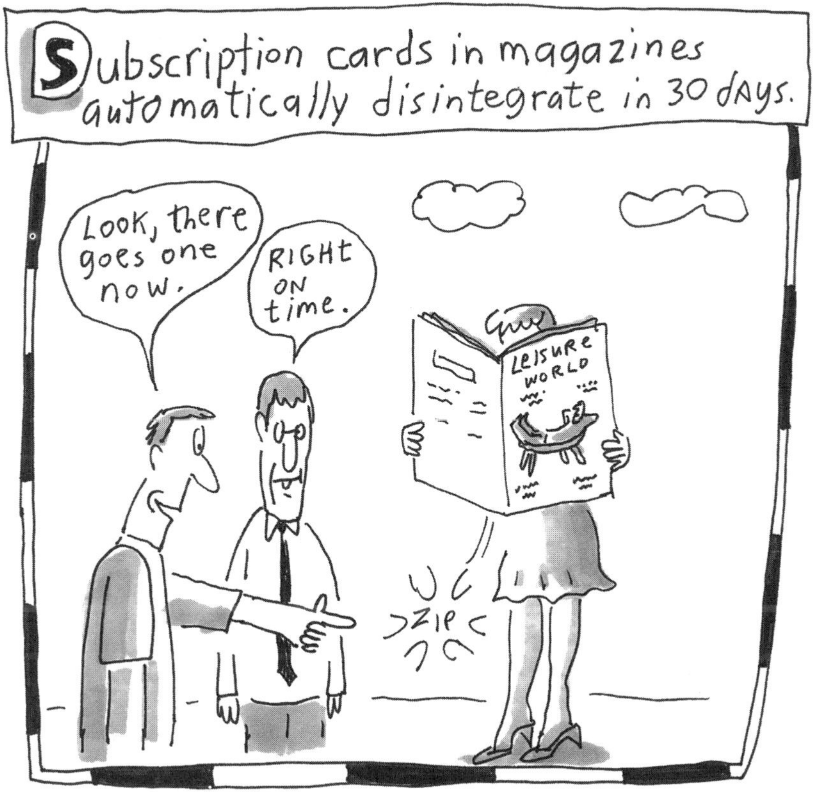
Subscription cards in magazines automatically disintegrate in 30 DAYS.
LOOK, there goes one now.
RIGHT ON time.
LEISURE WORLD
ZIP

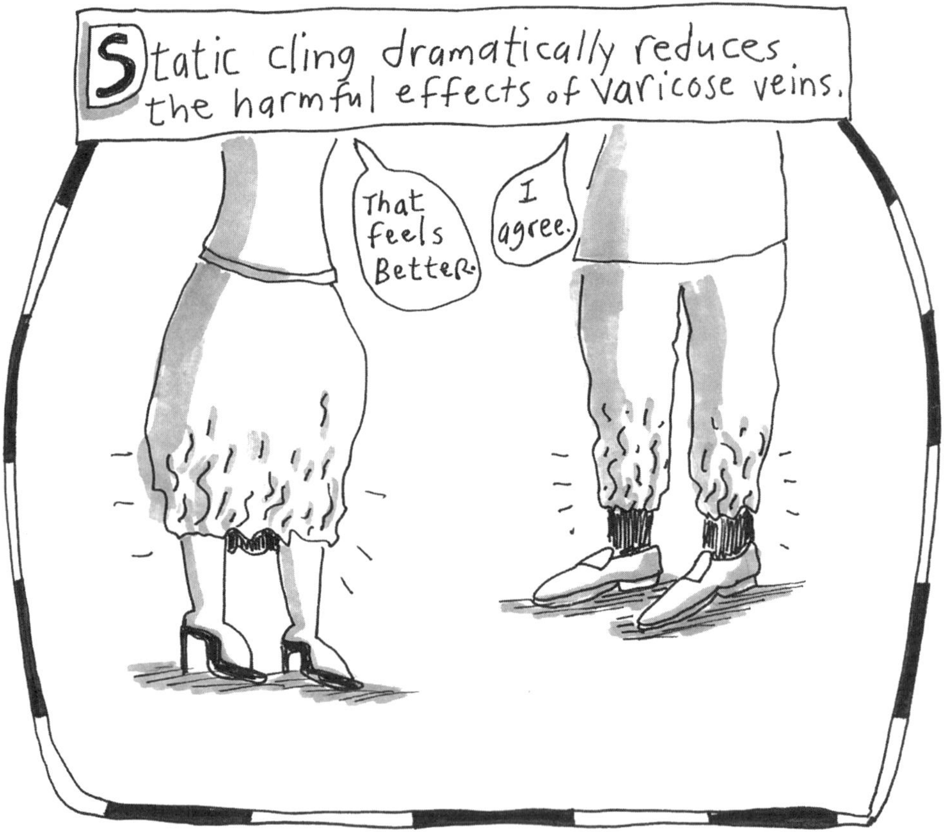
Static cling dramatically reduces the harmful effects of varicose veins.
That feels Better.
I agree.

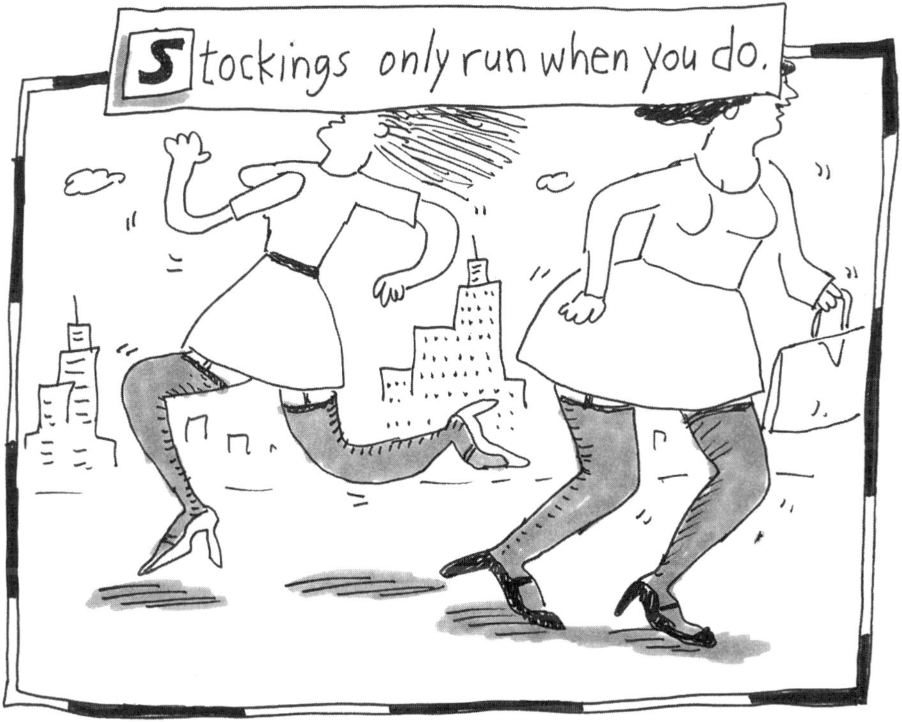
Stockings only run when you do.

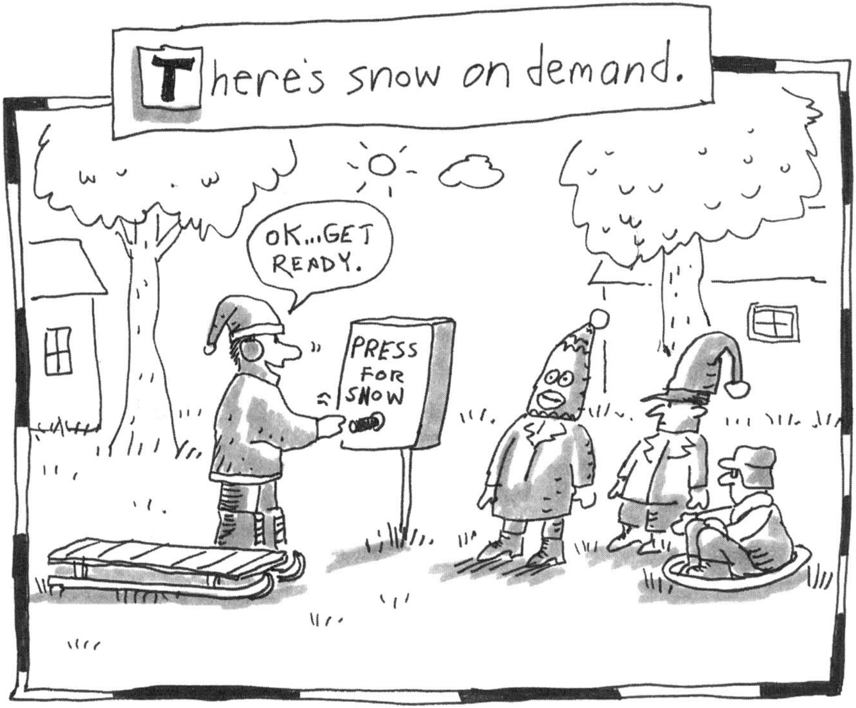
There's snow on demand.
OK...GET READY.
PRESS FOR SNOW

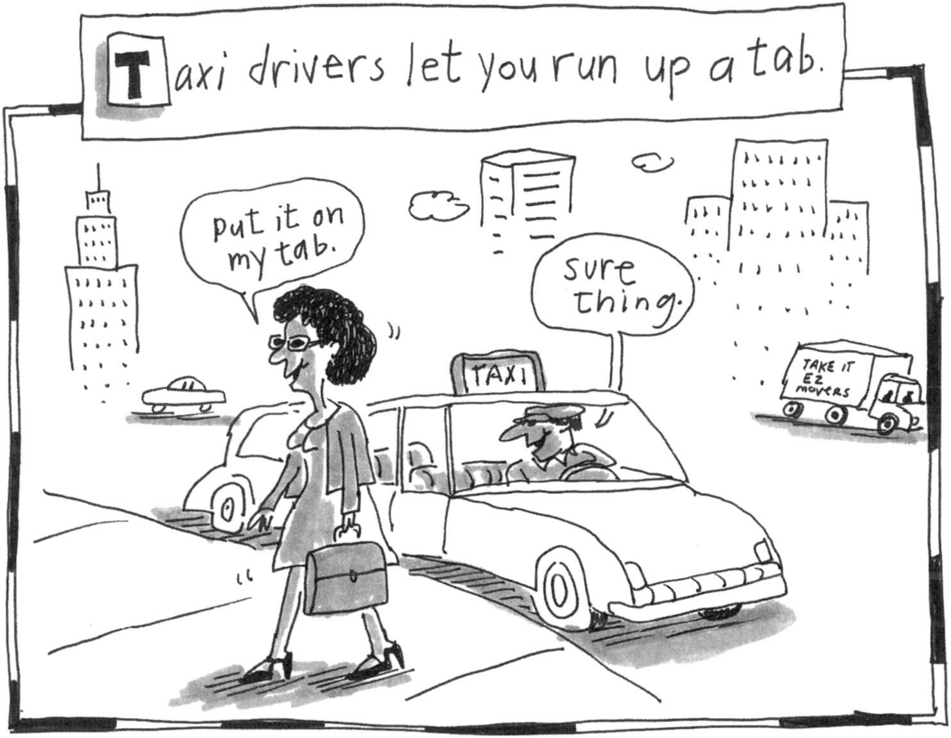
Taxi drivers let you run up a tab.
put it on my tab.
sure thing.
TAXI
TAKE IT EZ movers

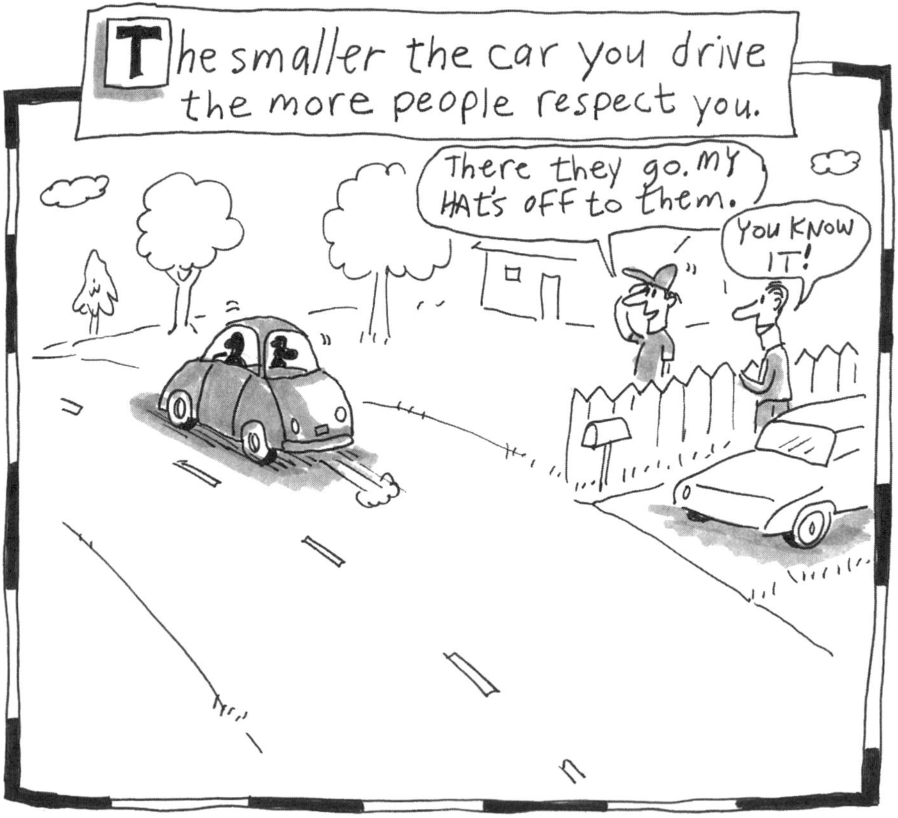
There they go. MY HAT's OFF to them.
YOU KNOW IT!

The smaller the car you drive the more people respect you.

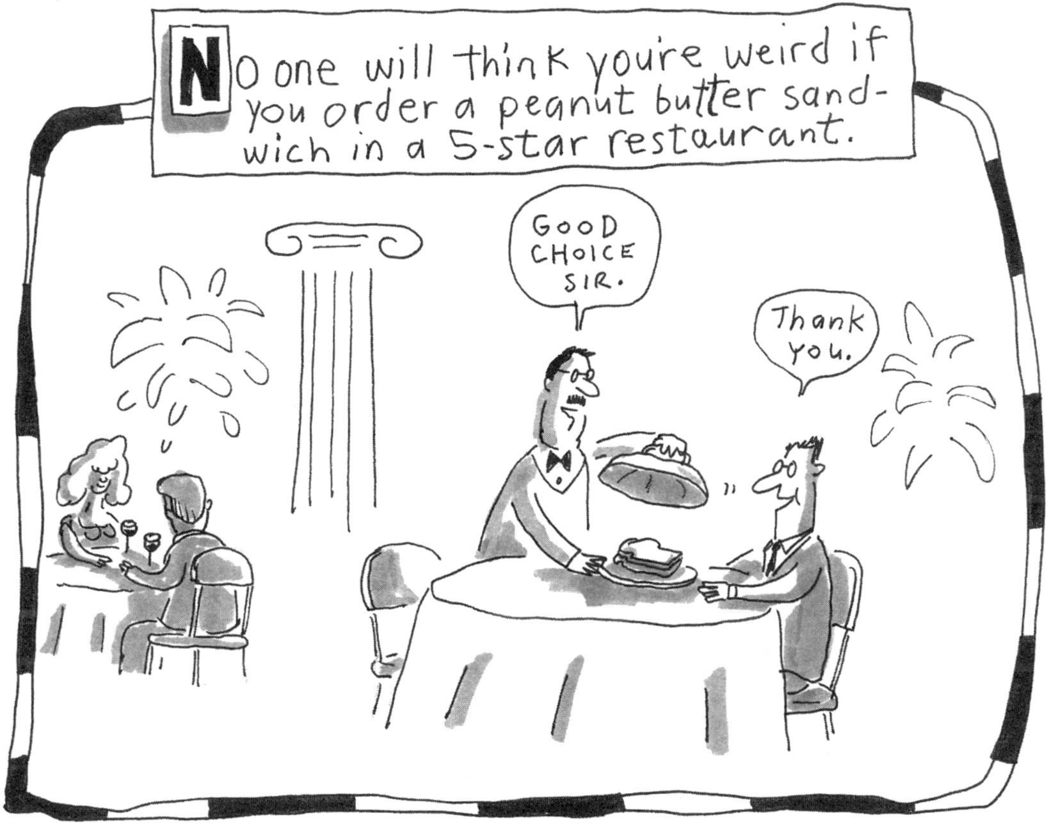
No one will think you're weird if you order a peanut butter sandwich in a 5-star restaurant.
GOOD CHOICE SIR.
Thank you.

12

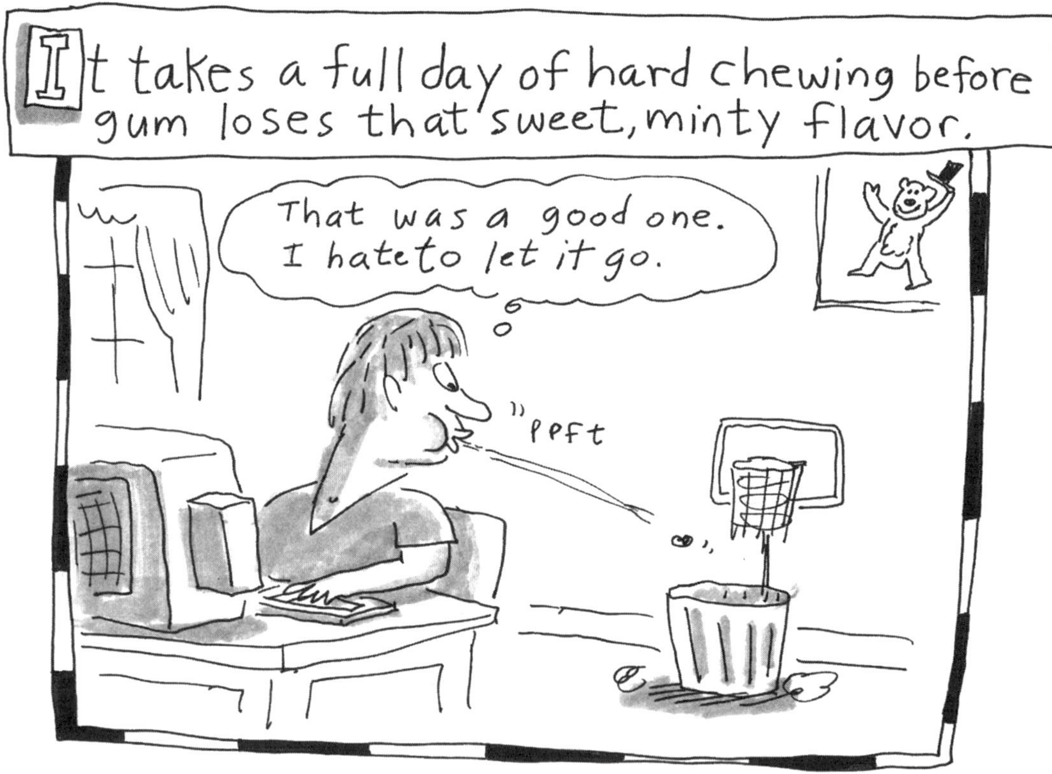
It takes a full day of hard chewing before gum loses that sweet, minty flavor.
That was a good one. I hate to let it go.
PPFT

Forests have biting, stinging, blood-sucking, creepy crawly free zones.

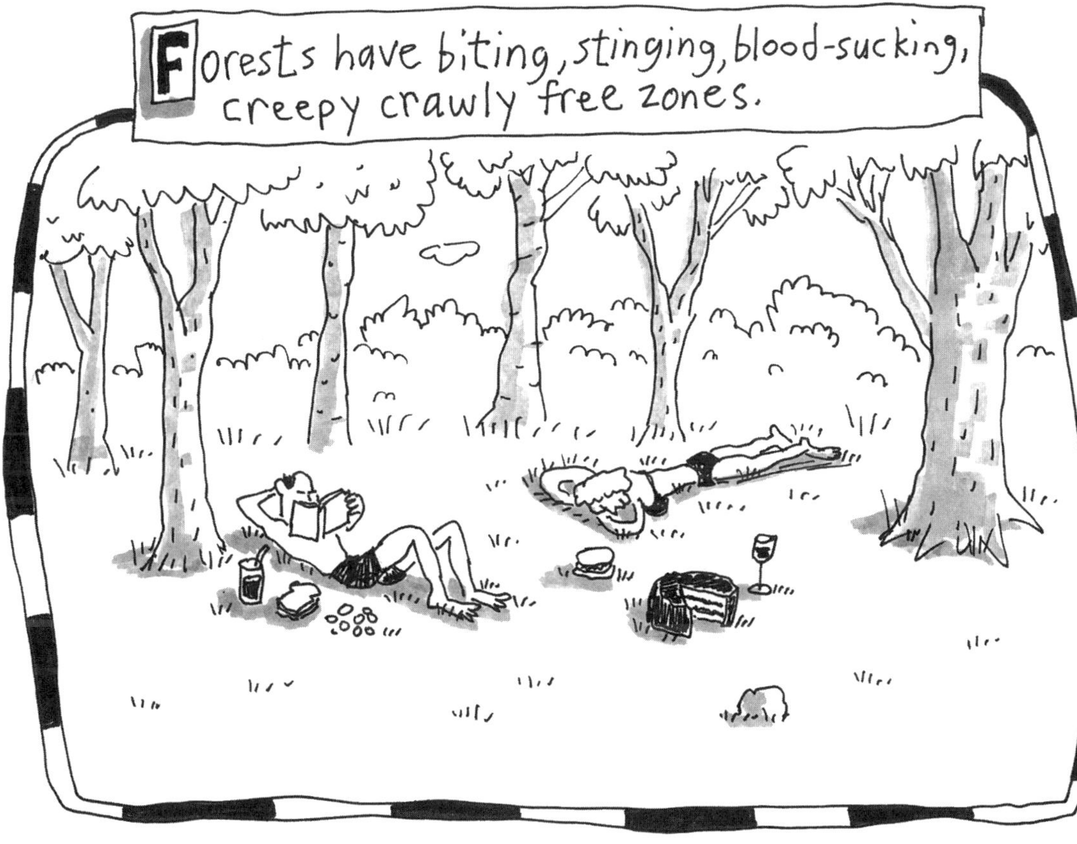

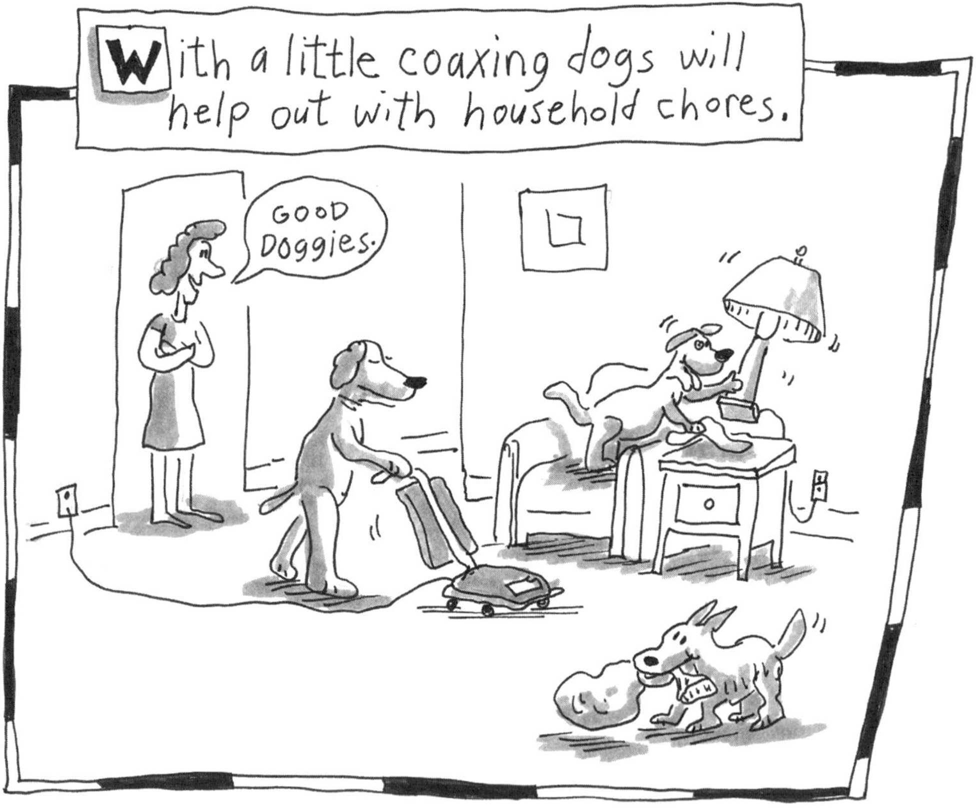
With a little coaxing dogs will help out with household chores.
GOOD Doggies.

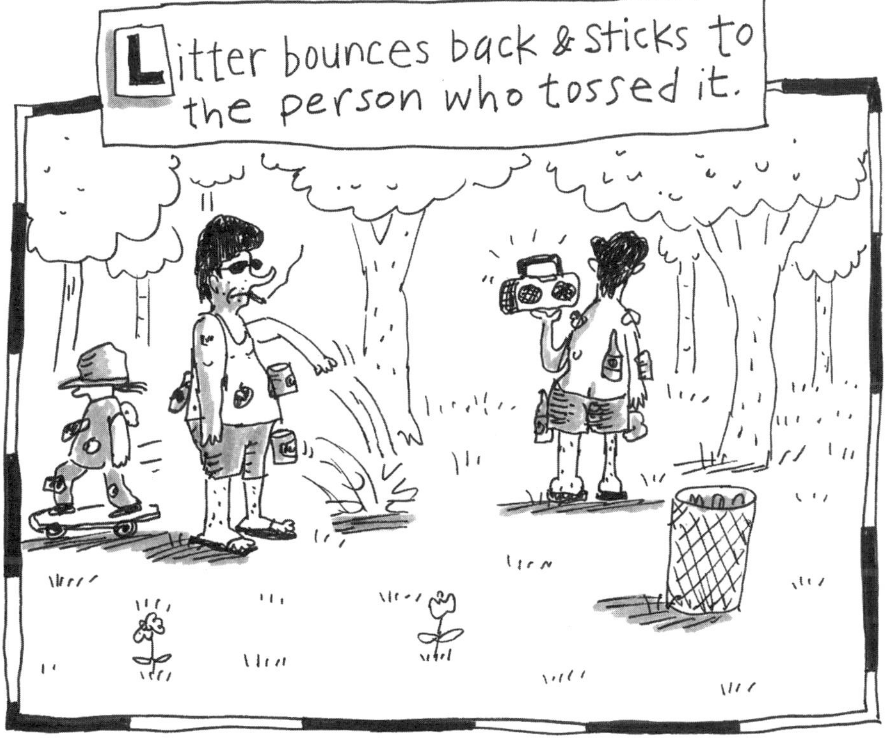
Litter bounces back & sticks to the person who tossed it.

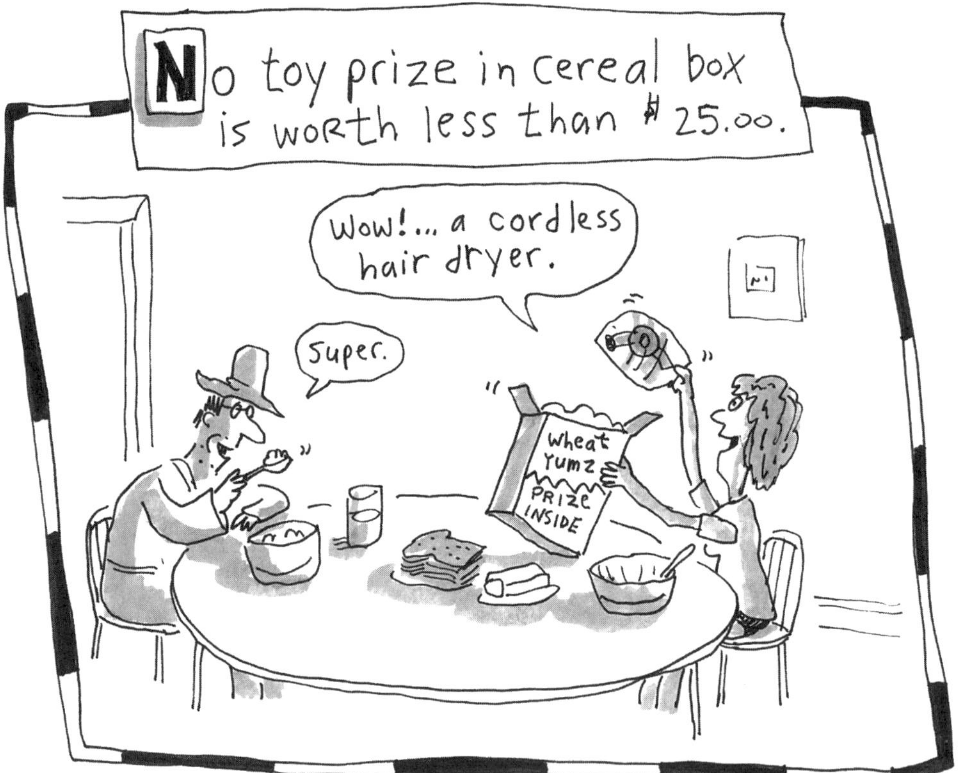
No toy prize in cereal box is worth less than $25.00.
Wow!... a cordless hair dryer.
Super.
Wheat Yumz
PRIZE INSIDE

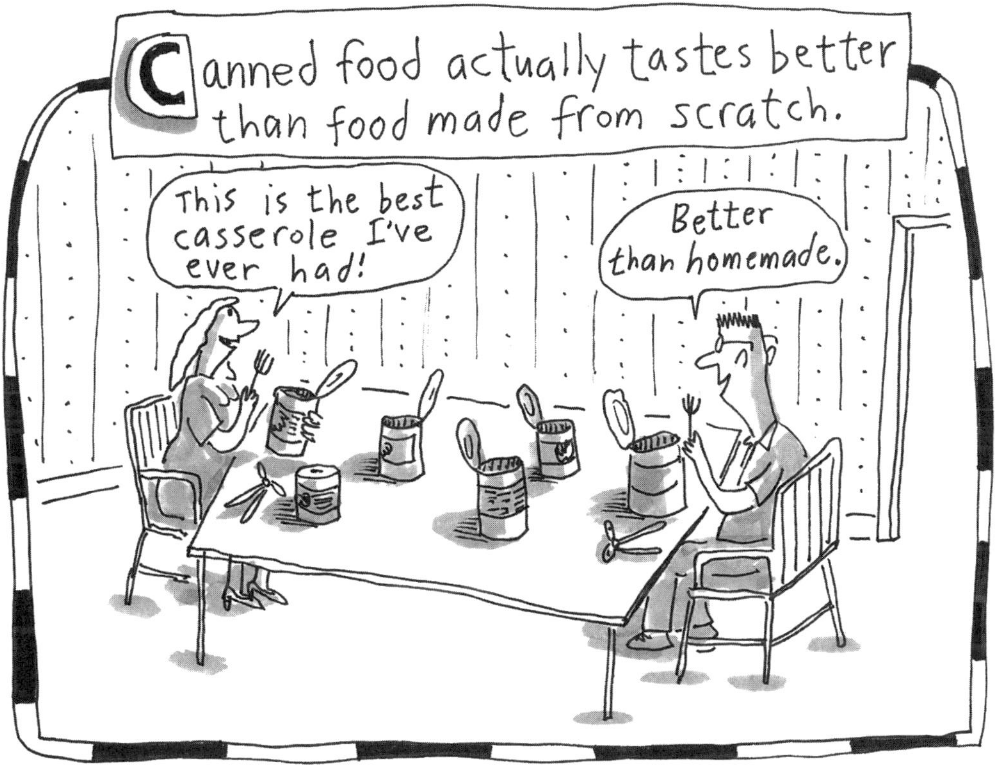
Canned food actually tastes better than food made from scratch.
This is the best casserole I've ever had!
Better than homemade.

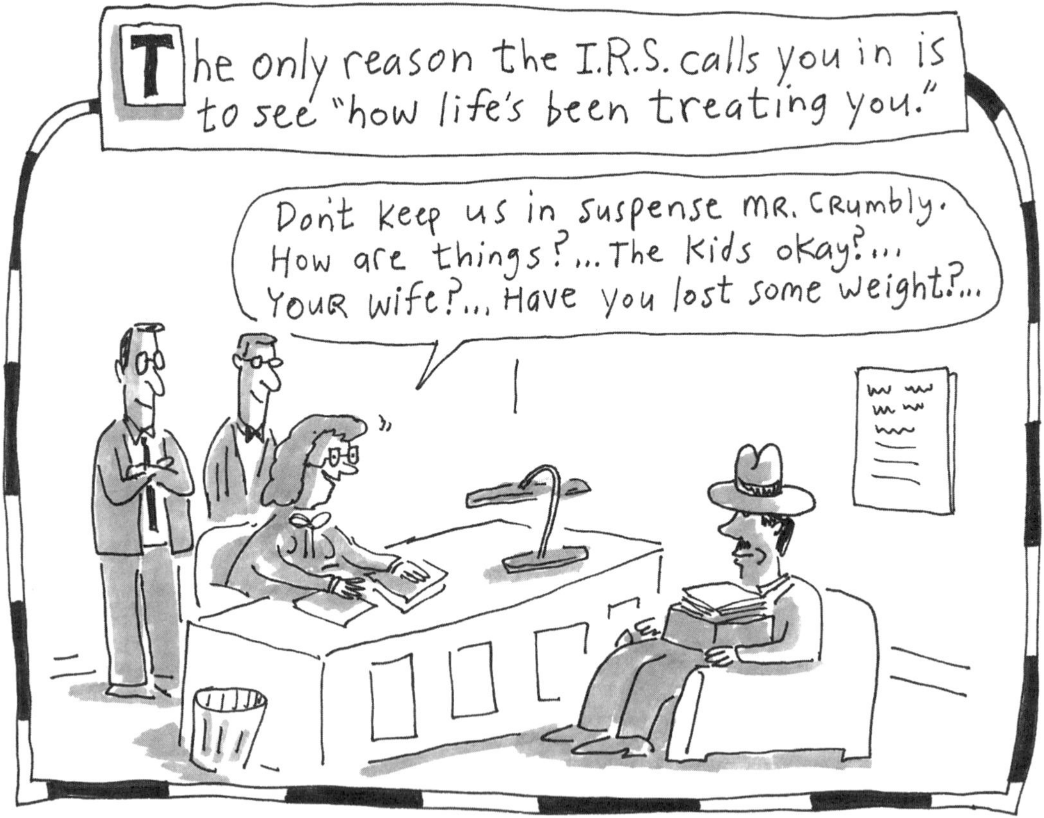
The only reason the I.R.S. calls you in is to see "how life's been treating you."
Don't keep us in suspense MR. CRumbly. How are things?... The Kids okay?... YOUR wife?... Have you lost some weight?...

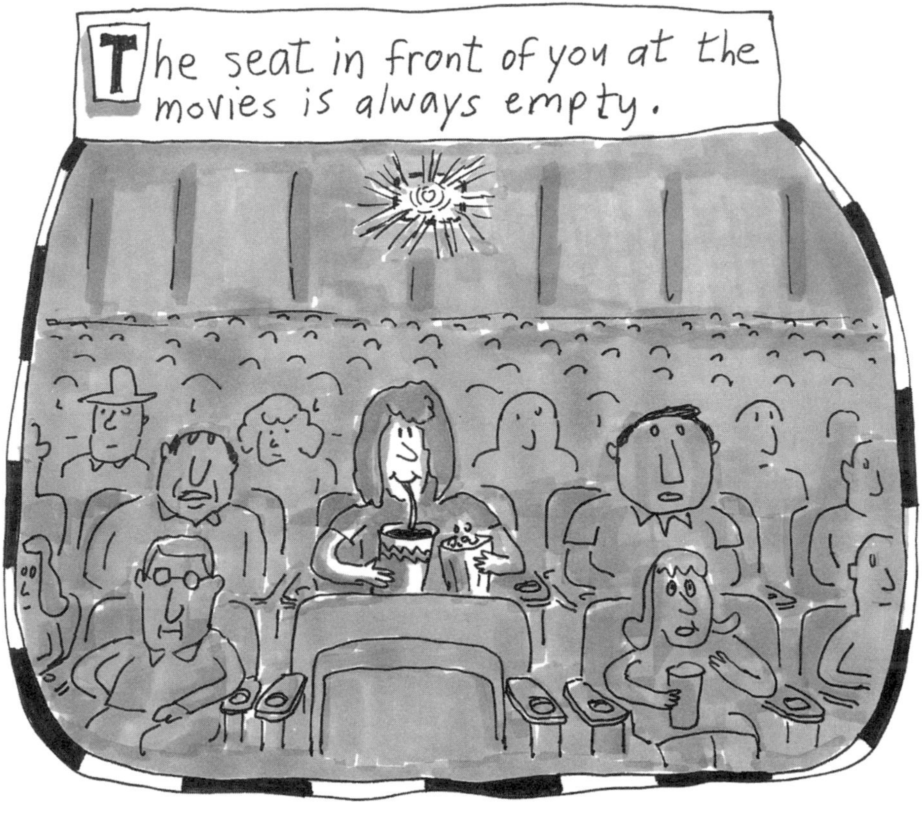
The seat in front of you at the movies is always empty.

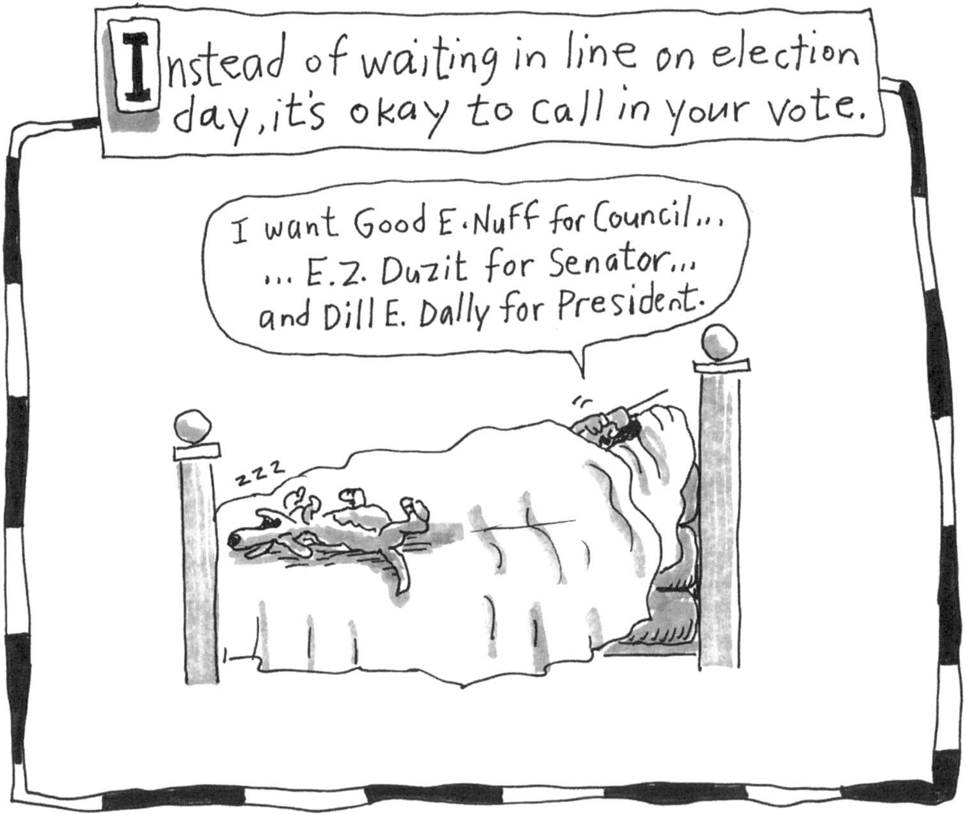
Instead of waiting in line on election day, it's okay to call in your vote.
I want Good E. Nuff for Council... ... E.Z. Duzit for Senator... and Dill E. Dally for President.
zzz

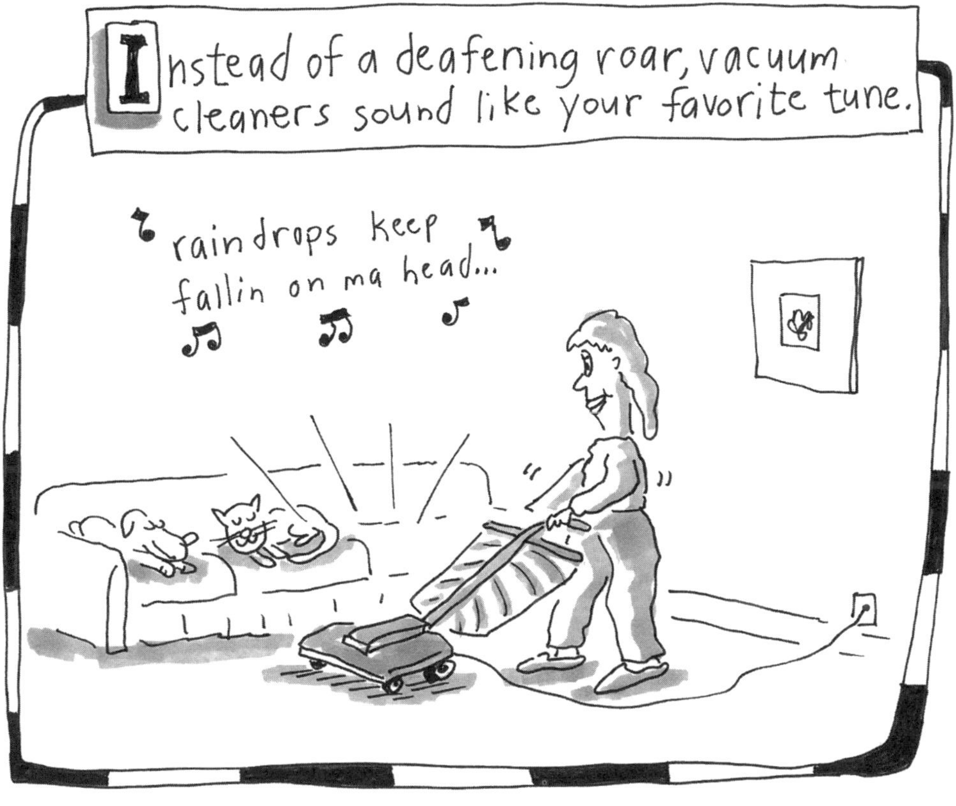
Instead of a deafening roar, vacuum cleaners sound like your favorite tune.
raindrops keep fallin on ma head...

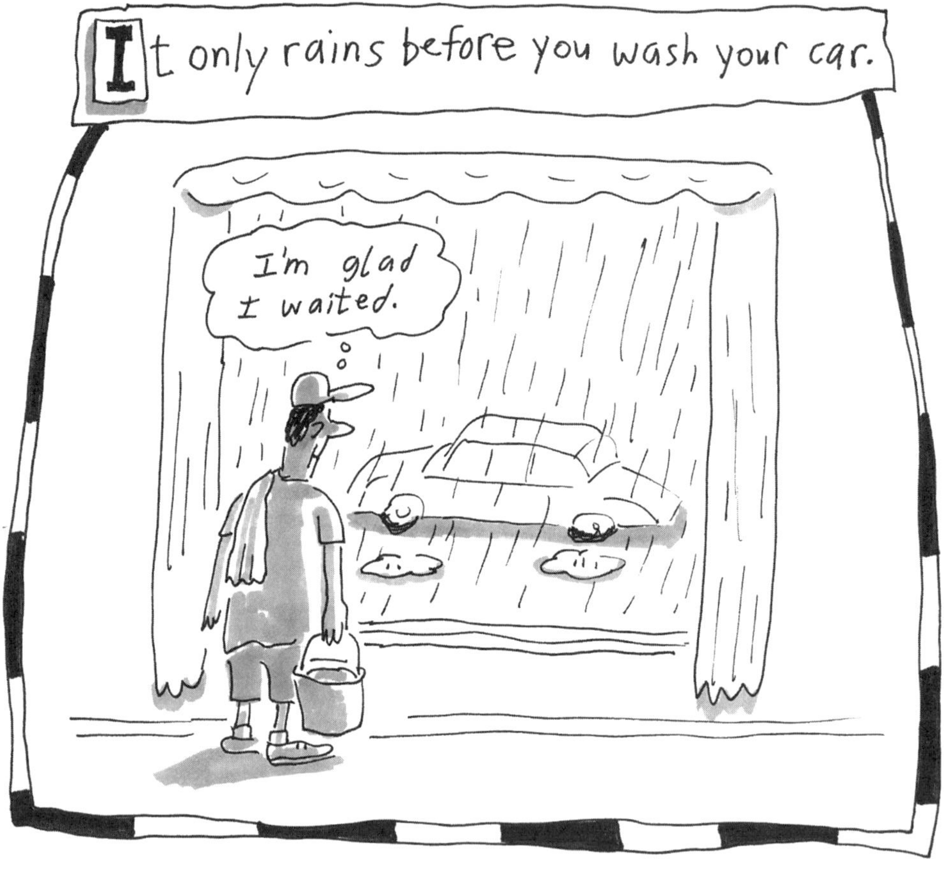
It only rains before you wash your car.
I'm glad I waited.

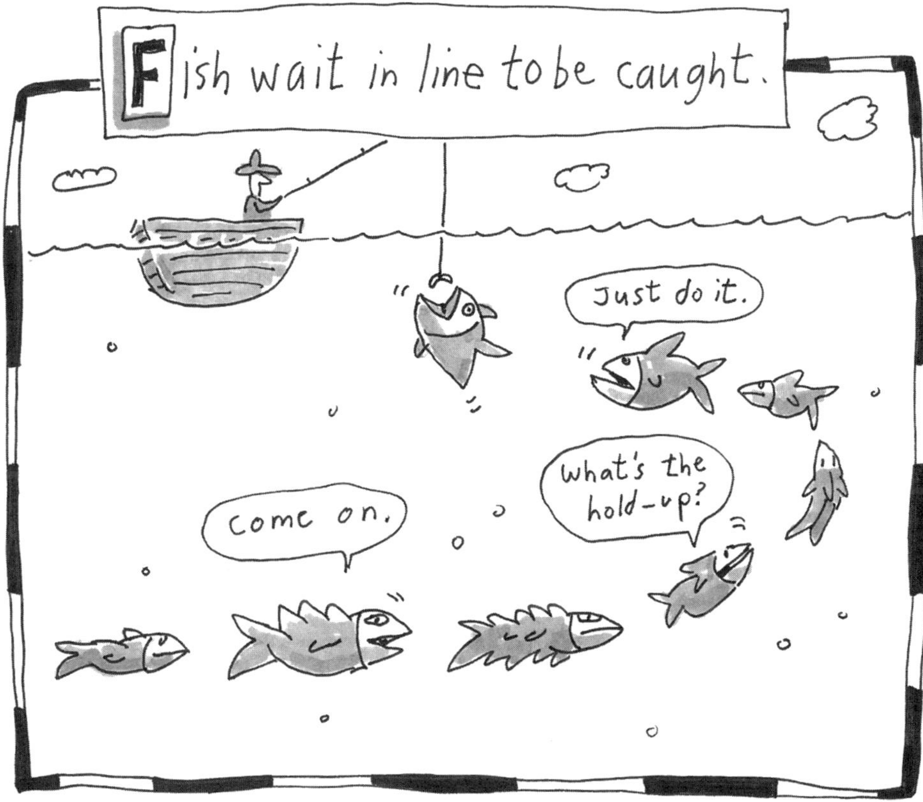
Fish wait in line to be caught.
Just do it.
What's the hold-up?
Come on.

23

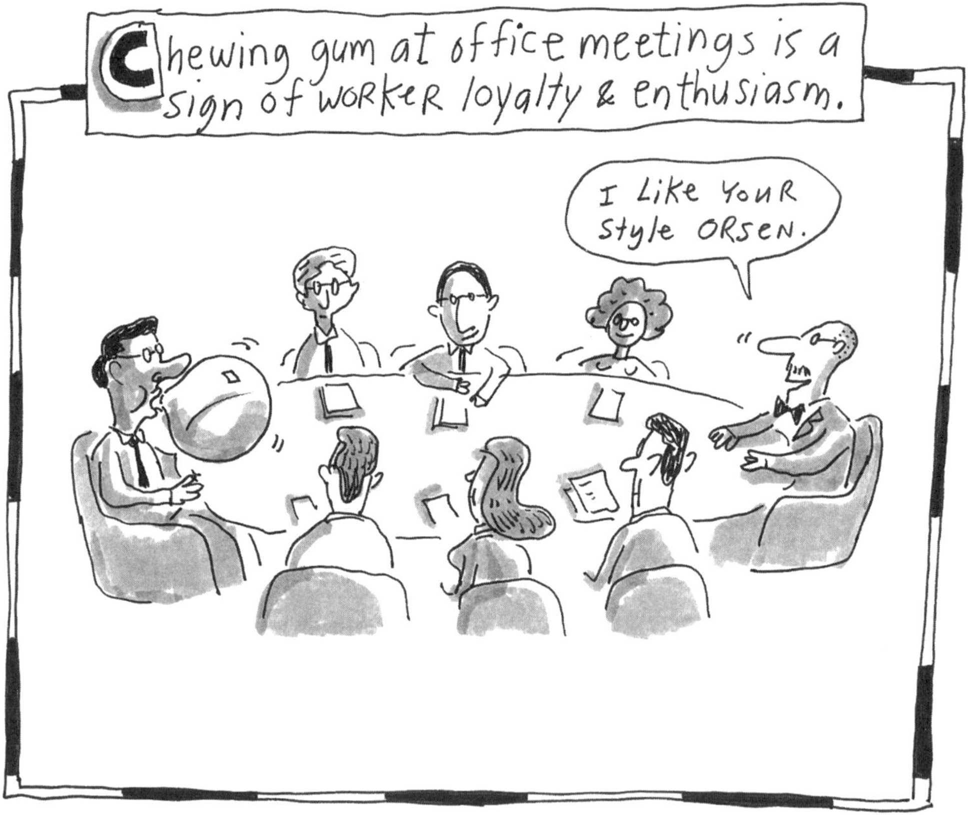
Chewing gum at office meetings is a sign of worker loyalty & enthusiasm.
I LIKE YOUR style ORSEN.

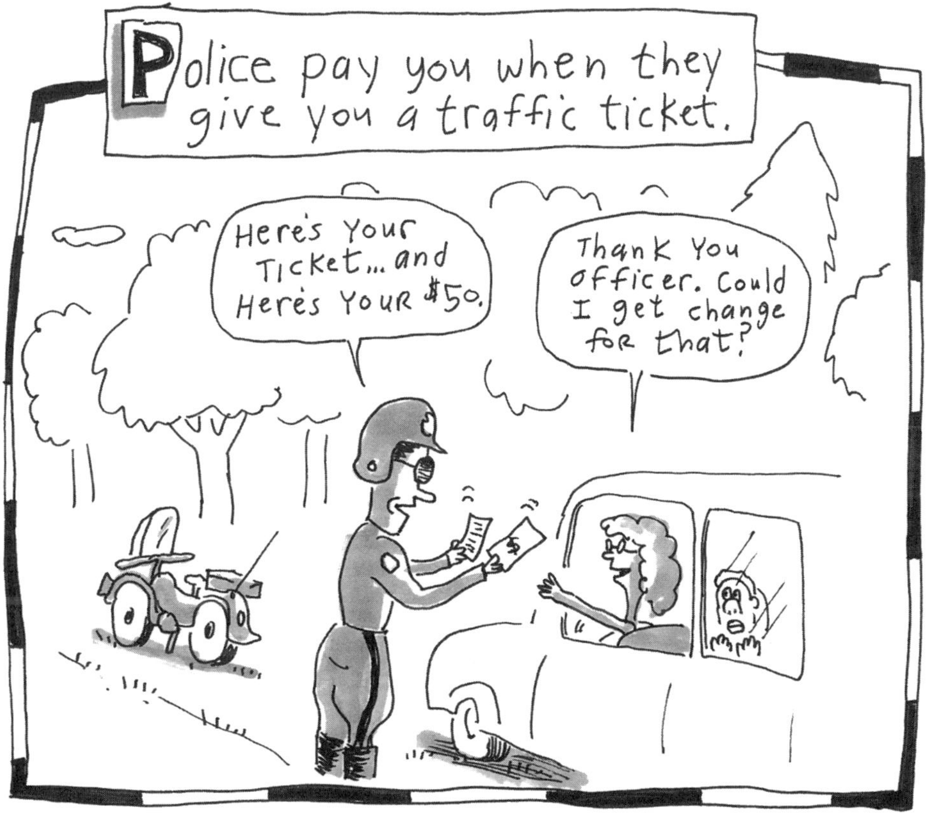
Police pay you when they give you a traffic ticket.
Here's your Ticket... and Here's your $50.
Thank you officer. Could I get change for that?

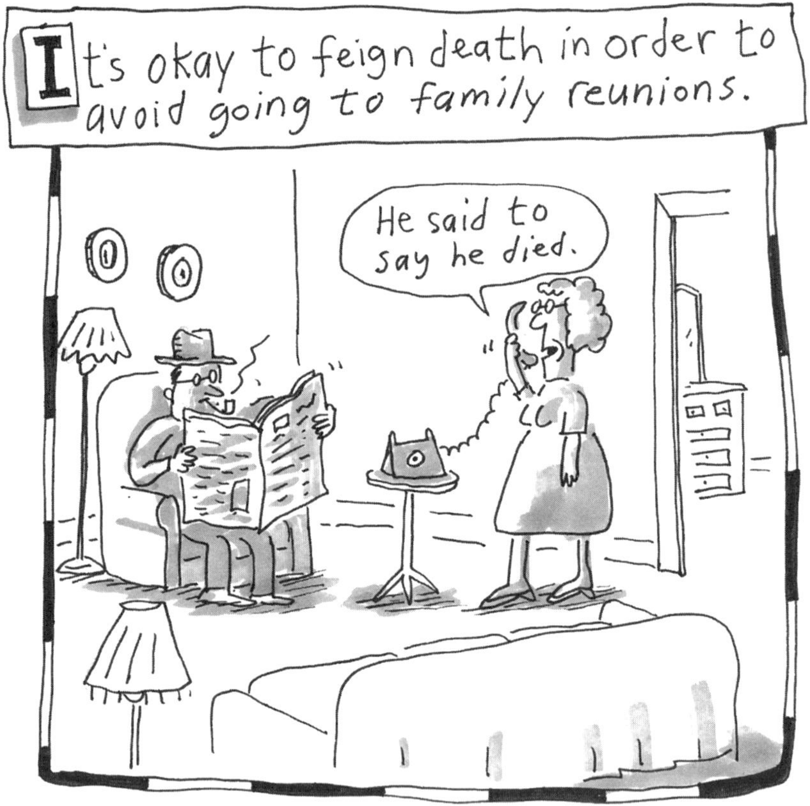
It's okay to feign death in order to avoid going to family reunions.
He said to say he died.

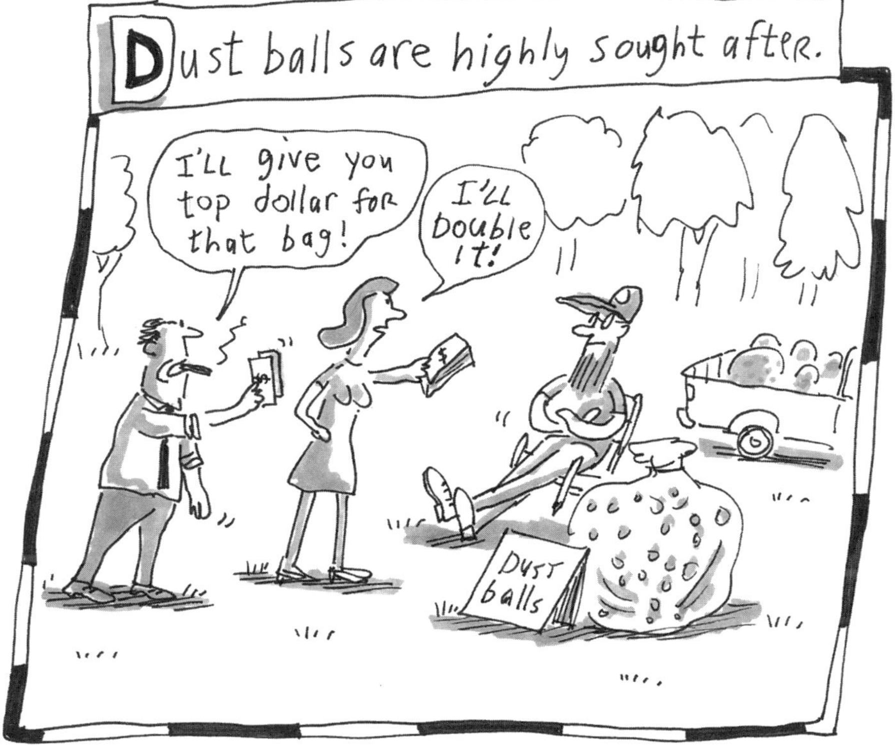
Dust balls are highly sought after.
I'LL give you top dollar for that bag!
I'LL Double it!
DUST balls

28

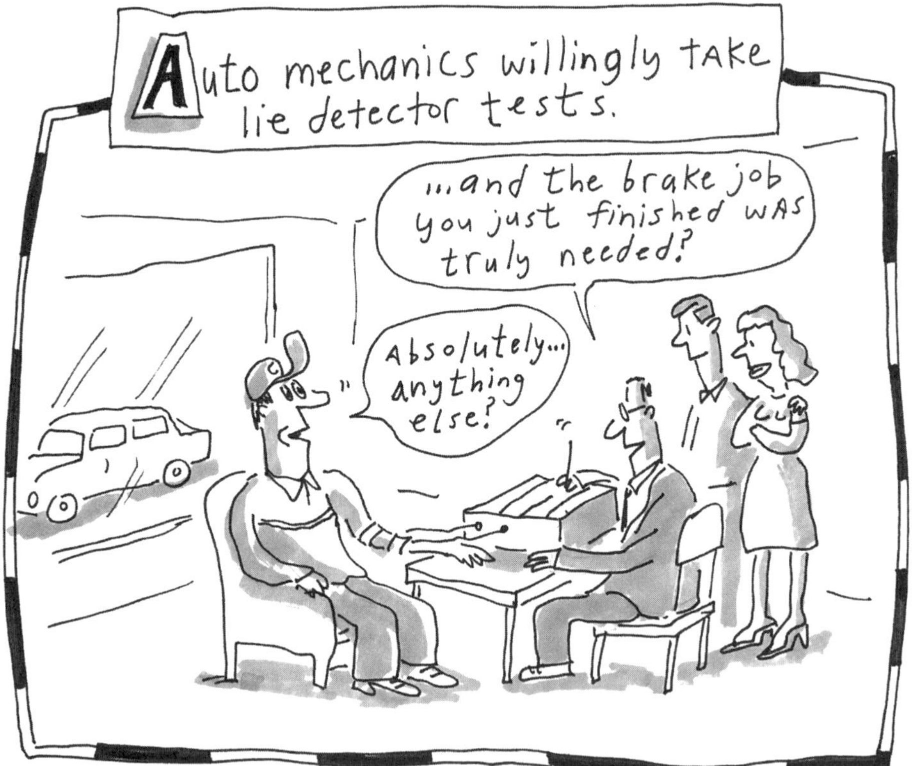
Auto mechanics willingly take lie detector tests.
...and the brake job you just finished WAS truly needed?
Absolutely... anything else?

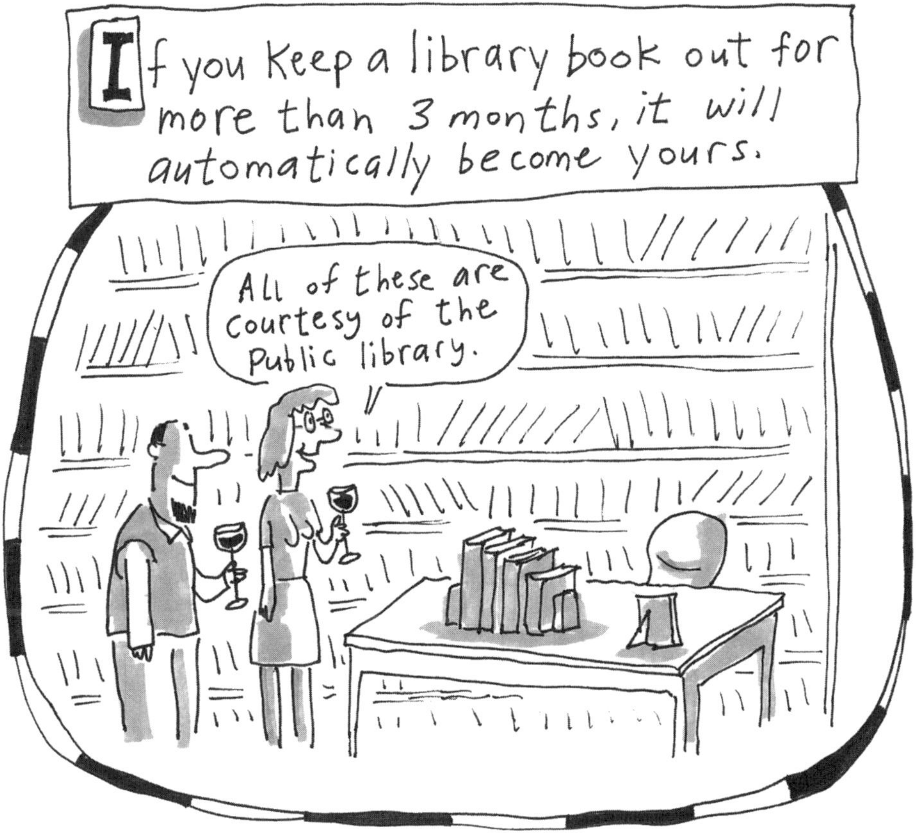
If you keep a library book out for more than 3 months, it will automatically become yours.
All of these are courtesy of the public library.

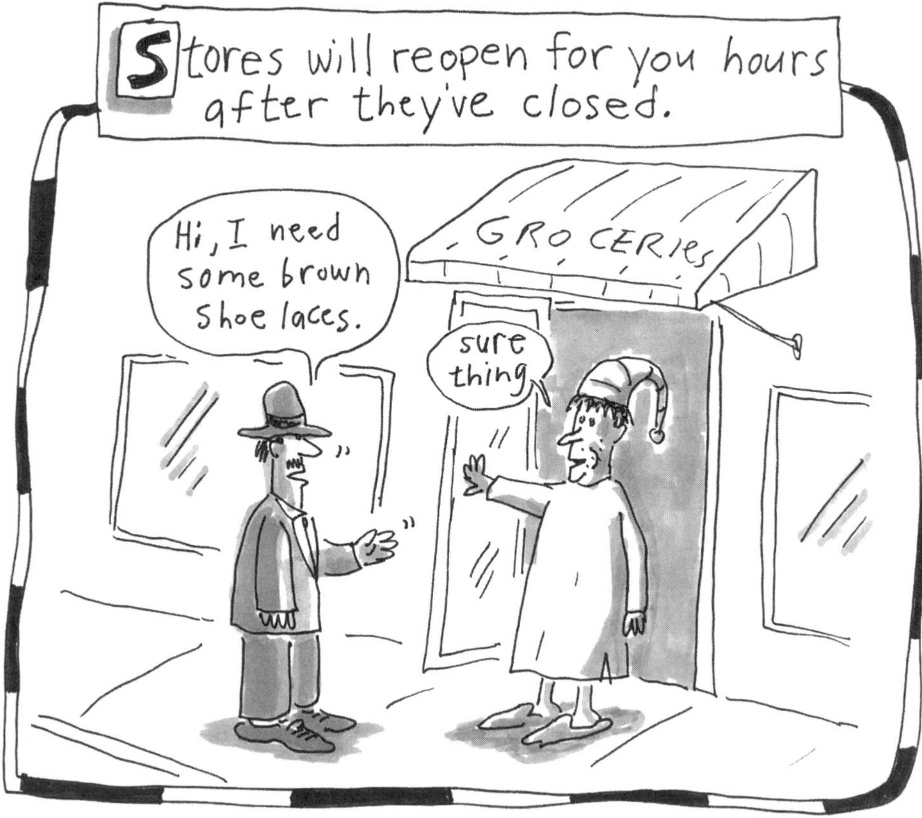
Stores will reopen for you hours after they've closed.
Hi, I need some brown shoe laces.
sure thing
GROCERIES

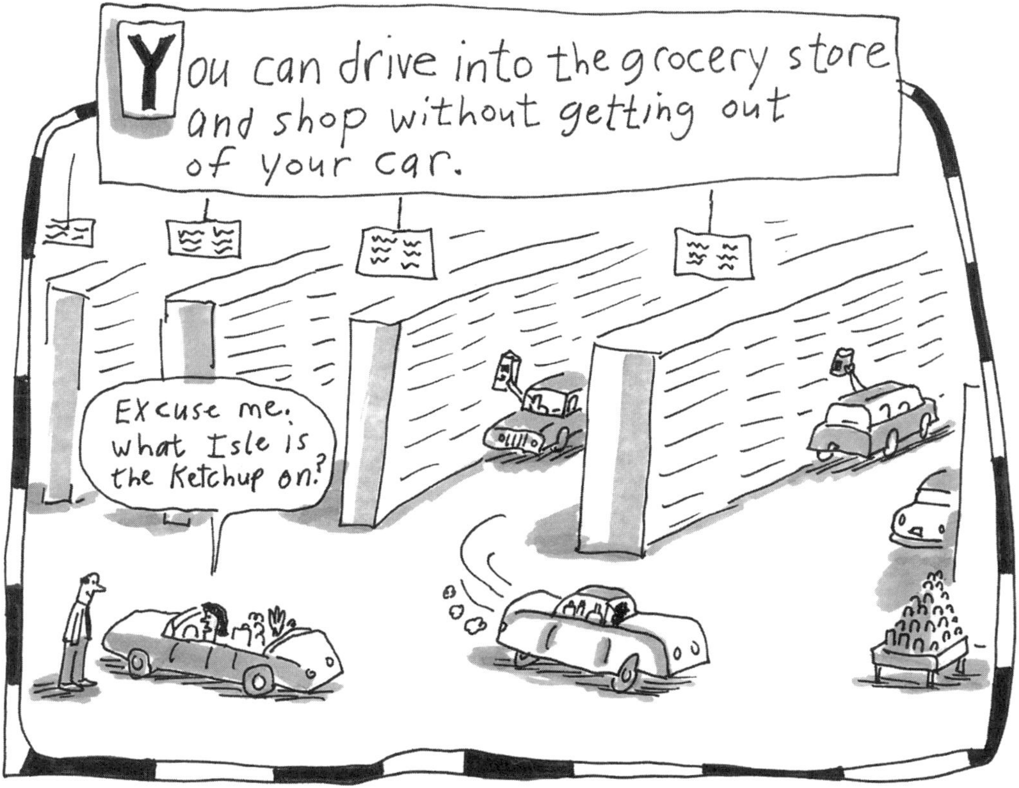
You can drive into the grocery store and shop without getting out of your car.
Excuse me. what Isle is the Ketchup on?

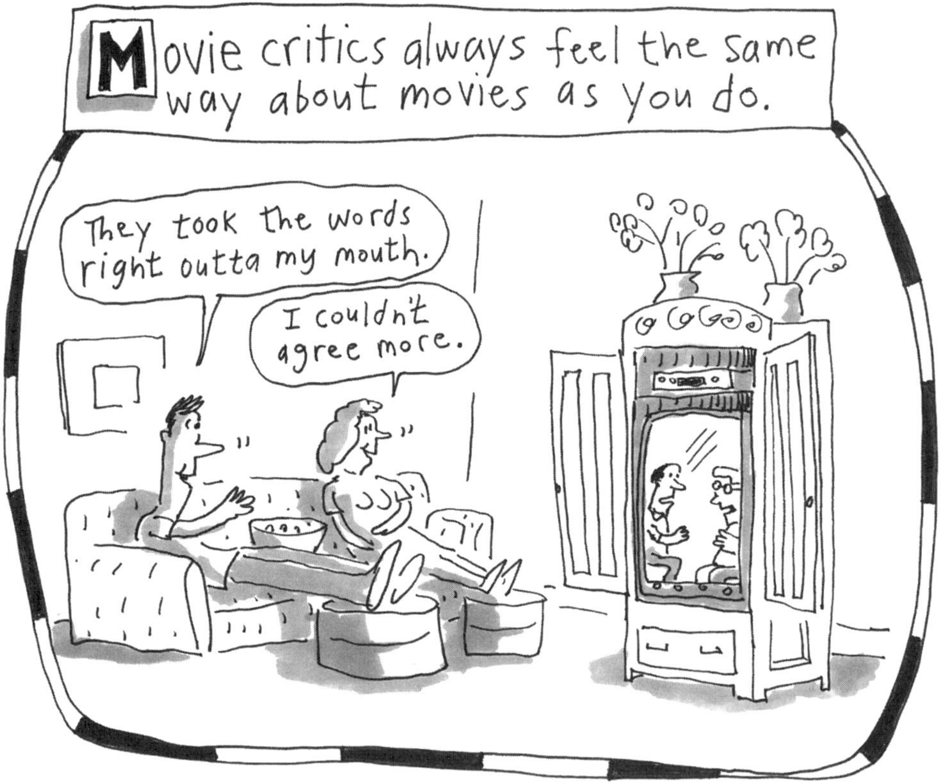
Movie critics always feel the same way about movies as you do.
They took the words right outta my mouth.
I couldn't agree more.

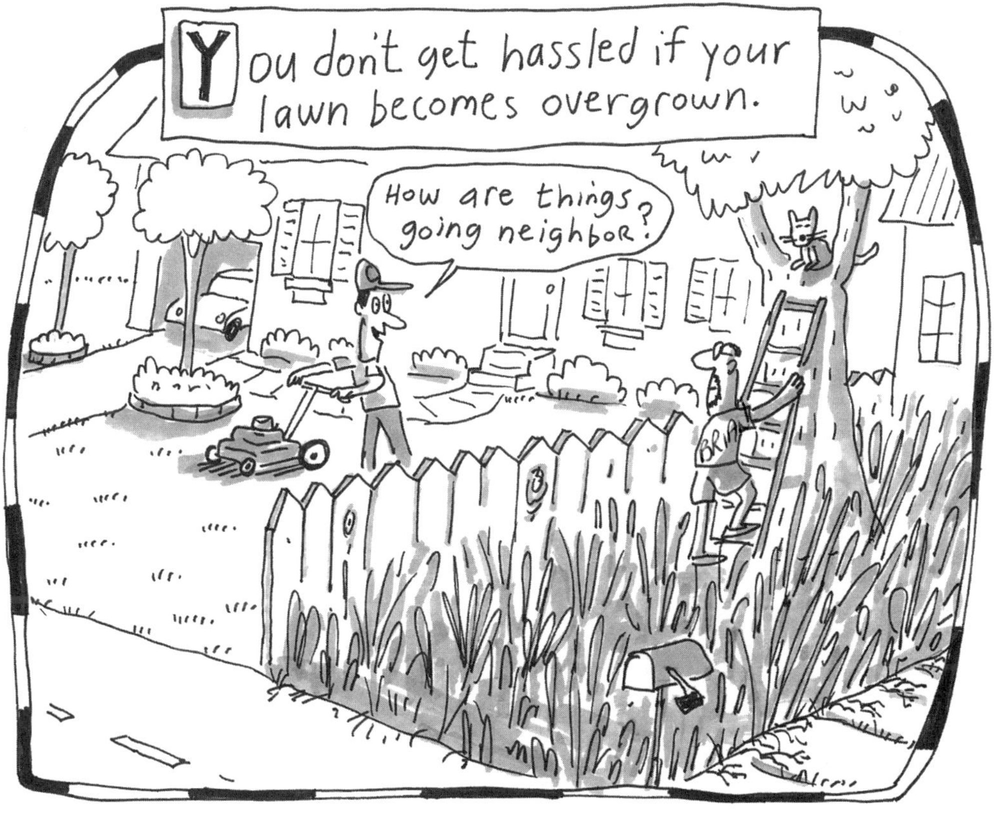
You don't get hassled if your lawn becomes overgrown.
How are things going neighbor?

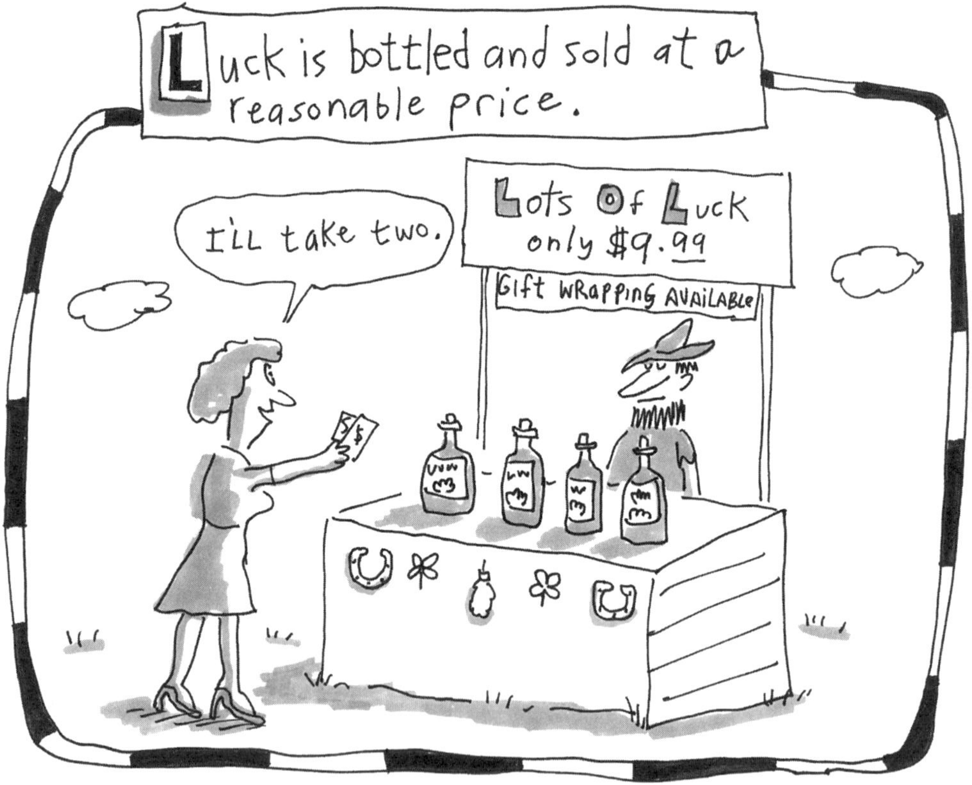
Luck is bottled and sold at a reasonable price.
I'll take two.
Lots Of Luck
only $9.99
Gift Wrapping Available

34

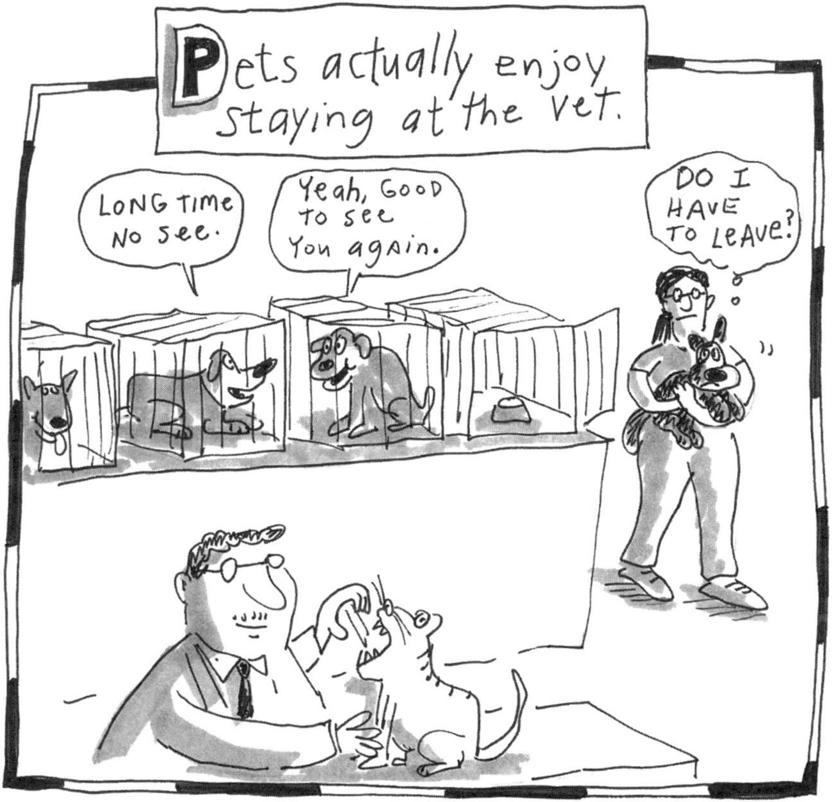
Pets actually enjoy staying at the vet.
LONG TIME NO SEE.
Yeah, GOOD TO SEE YOU AGAIN.
DO I HAVE TO LEAVE?

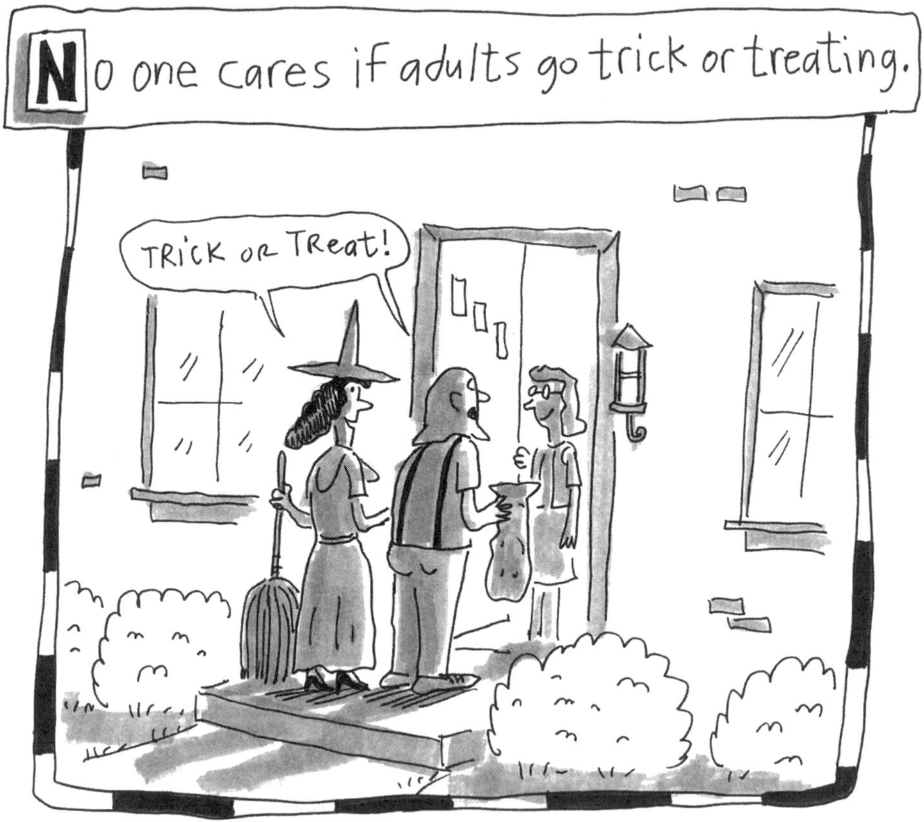
No one cares if adults go trick or treating.
TRICK OR TREAT!

36

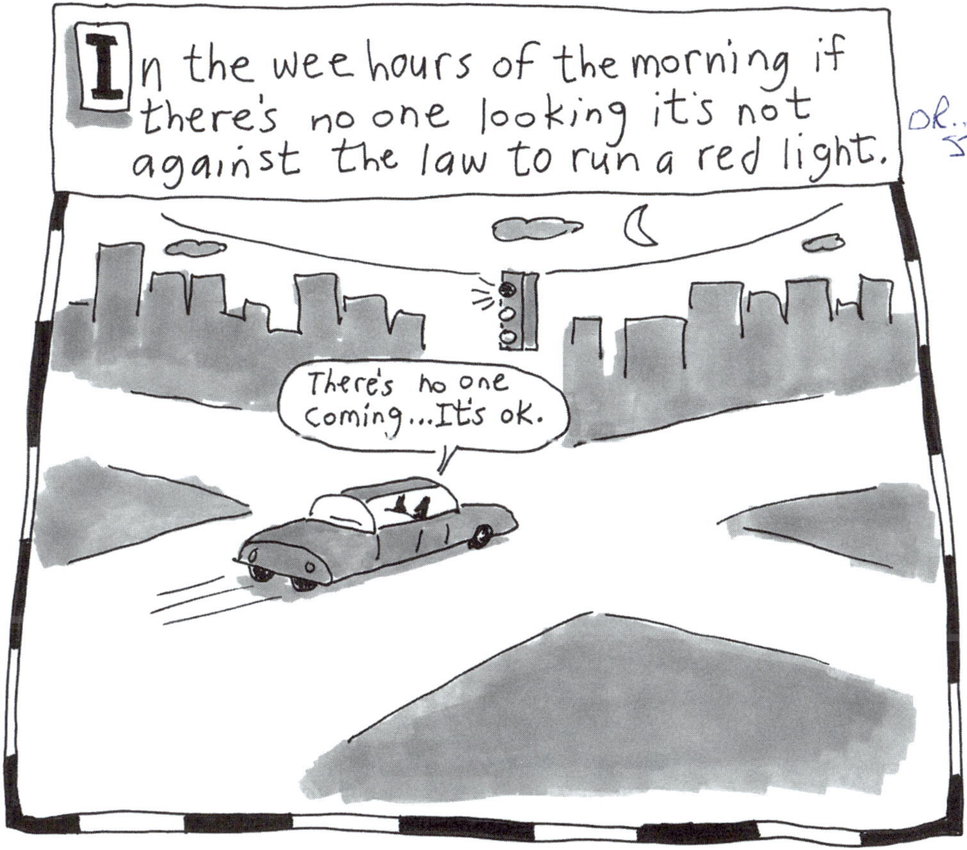
In the wee hours of the morning if there's no one looking it's not against the law to run a red light.
There's no one coming...It's ok.

OR... STOP SIGN

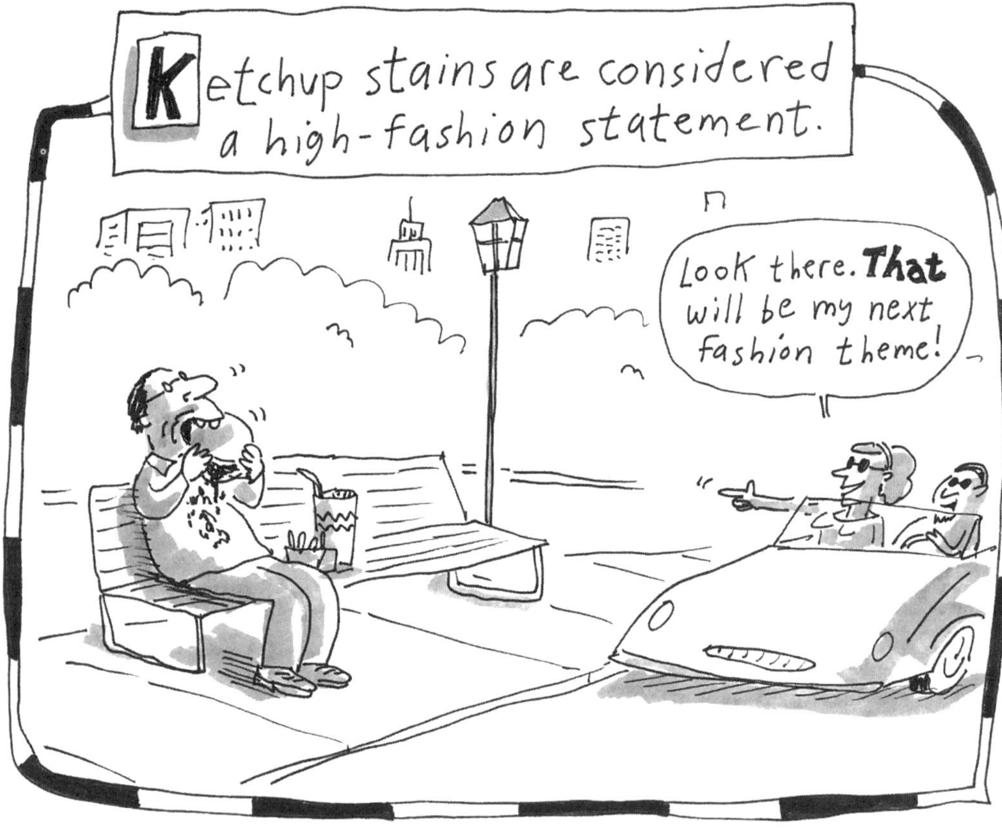
Ketchup stains are considered a high-fashion statement.
Look there. **That** will be my next fashion theme!

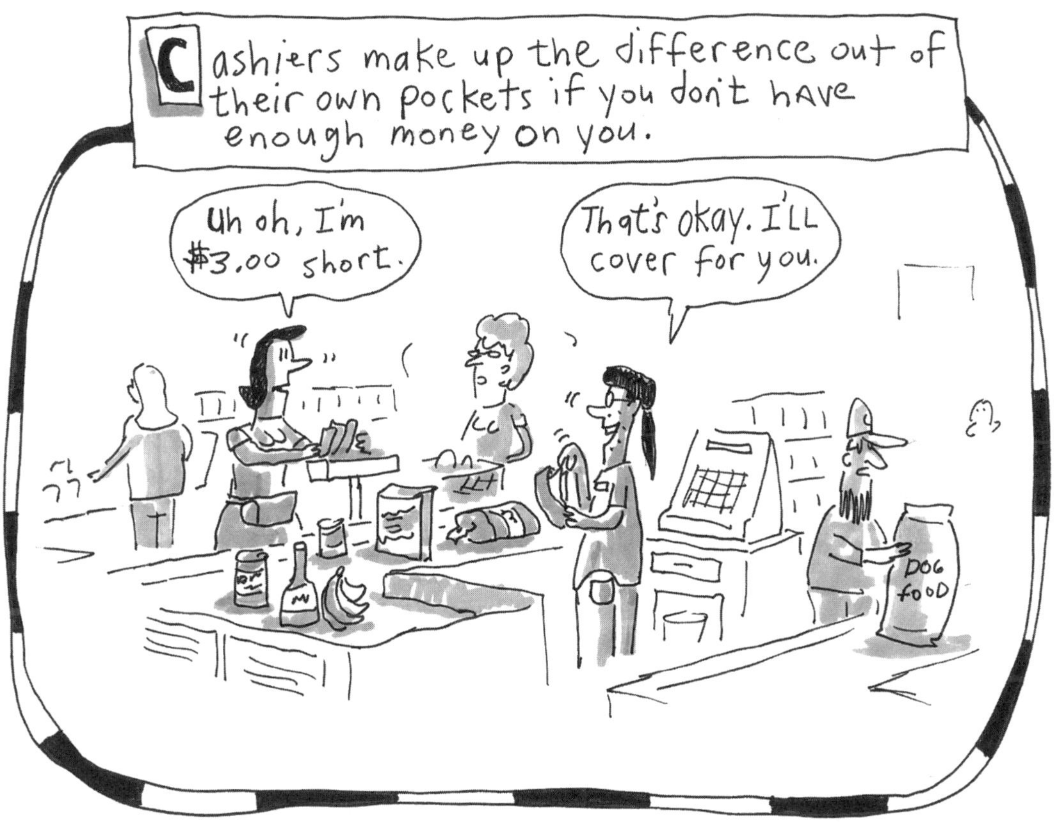
Cashiers make up the difference out of their own pockets if you don't have enough money on you.
Uh oh, I'm $3.00 short.
That's okay. I'll cover for you.
DOG FOOD

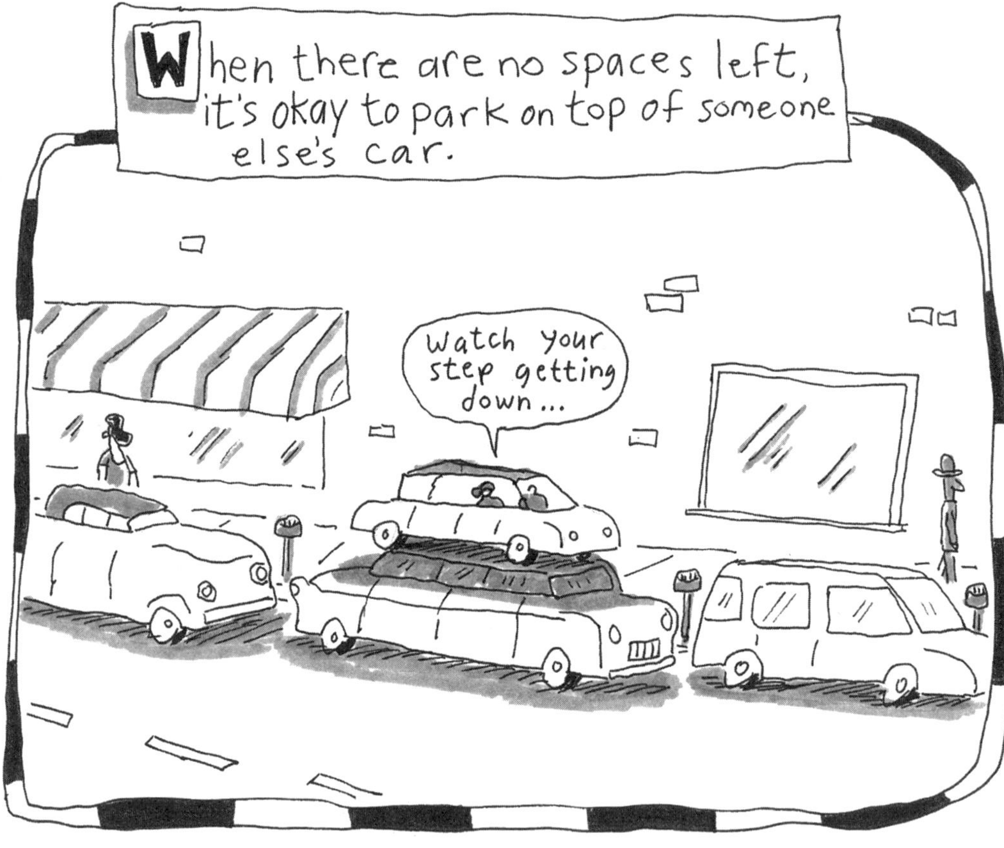
When there are no spaces left, it's okay to park on top of someone else's car.
Watch your step getting down...

40

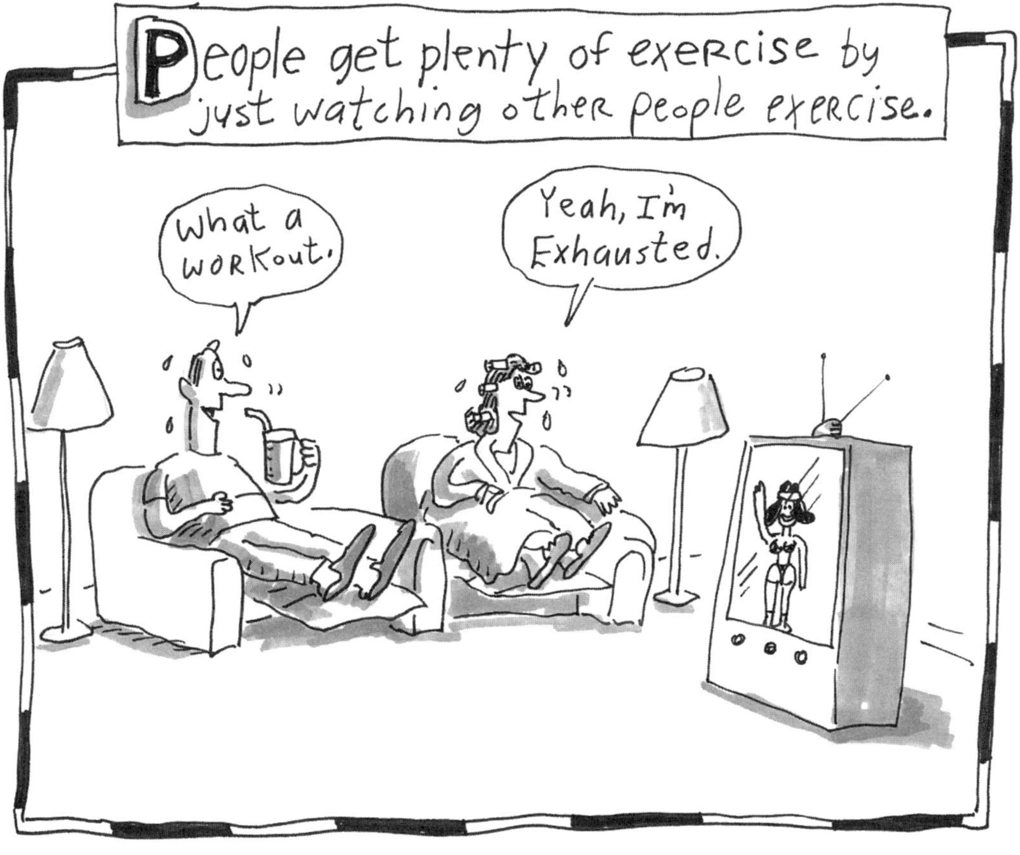
People get plenty of exercise by just watching other people exercise.
What a workout.
Yeah, I'm Exhausted.

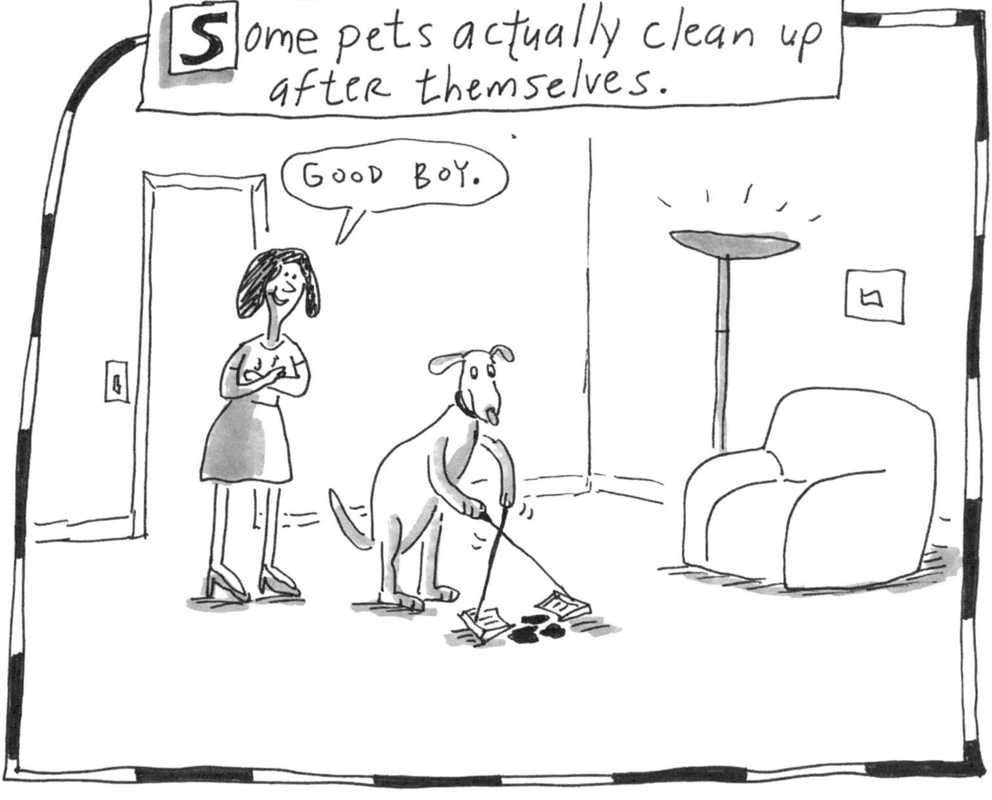
Some pets actually clean up after themselves.
GOOD BOY.

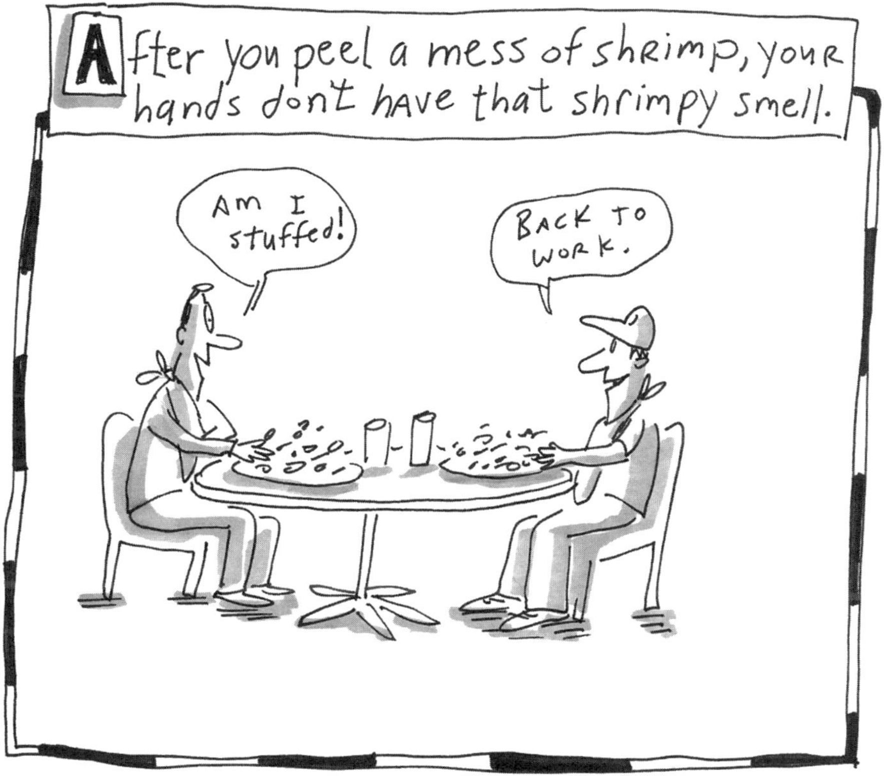
After you peel a mess of shrimp, your hands don't have that shrimpy smell.
Am I stuffed!
BACK TO WORK.

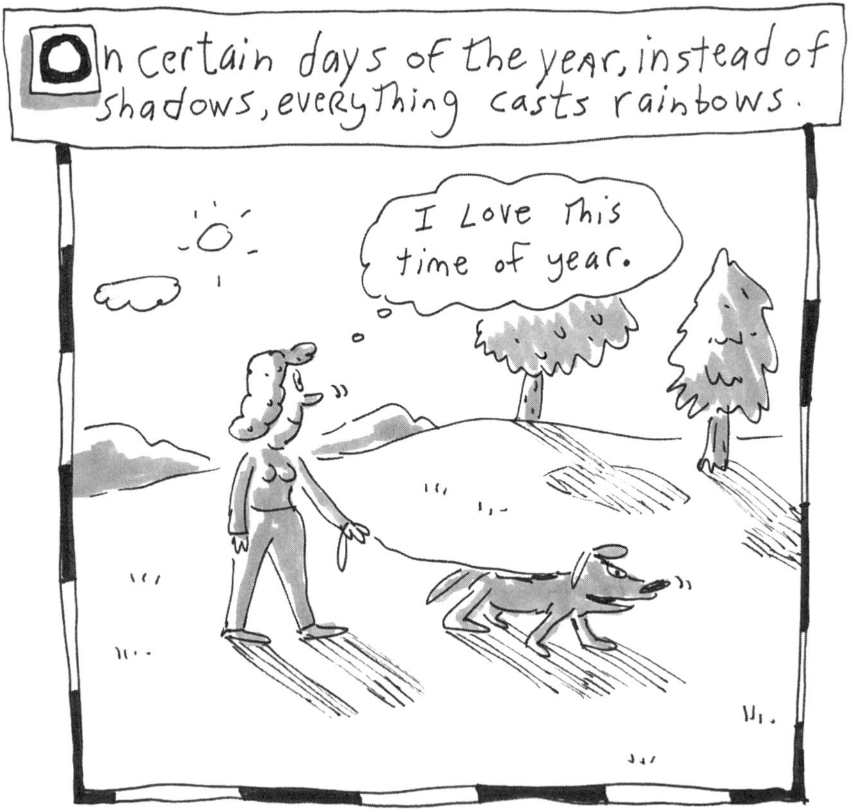
On certain days of the year, instead of shadows, everything casts rainbows.
I Love This time of year.

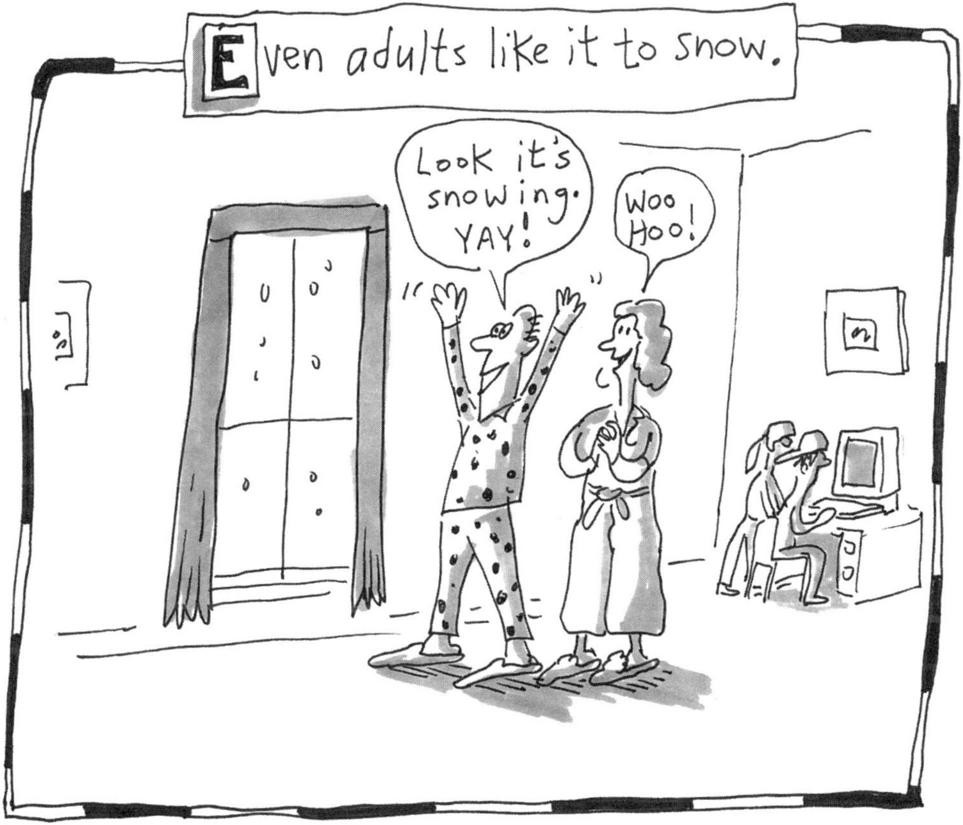
Even adults like it to snow.
Look it's snowing. YAY!
Woo Hoo!

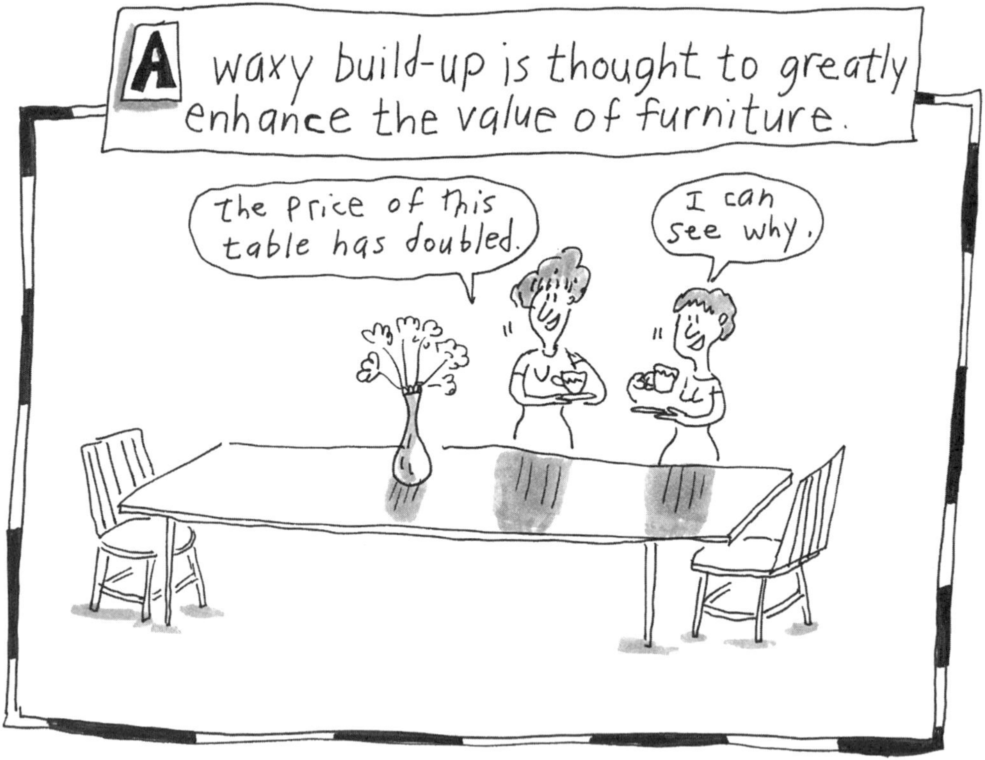
A waxy build-up is thought to greatly enhance the value of furniture.
The price of this table has doubled.
I can see why.

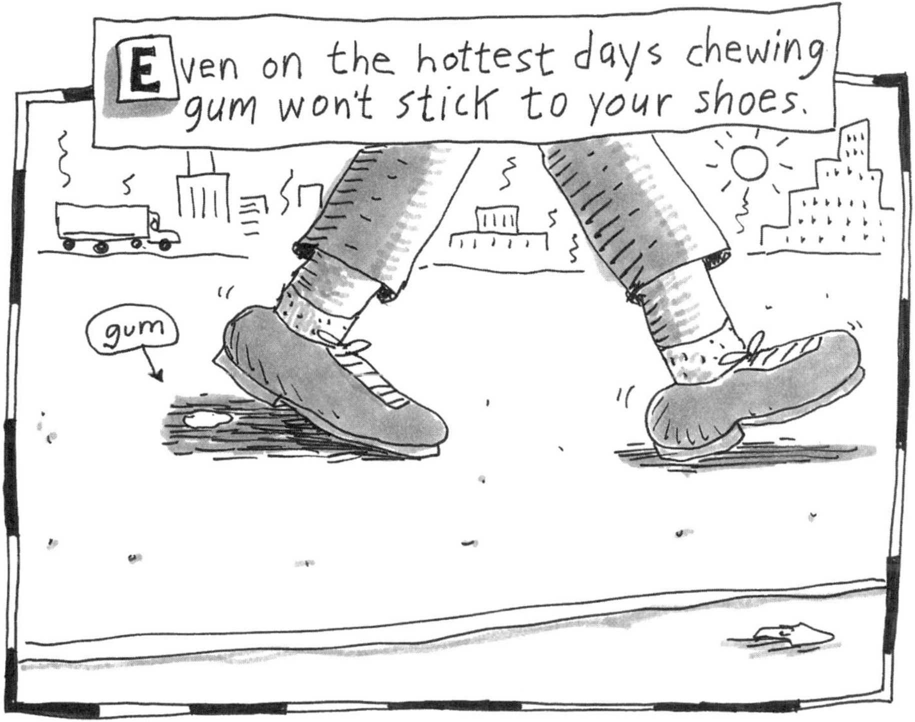
Even on the hottest days chewing gum won't stick to your shoes.
gum

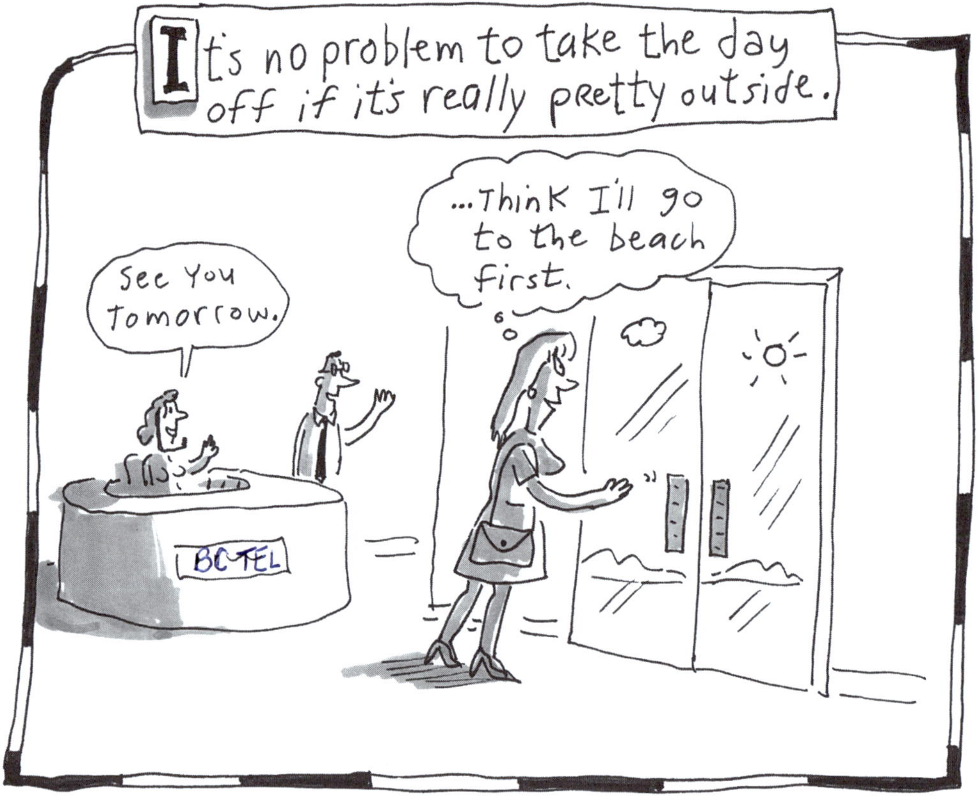
It's no problem to take the day off if it's really pretty outside.
...Think I'll go to the beach first.
See You Tomorrow.
BC TEL

48

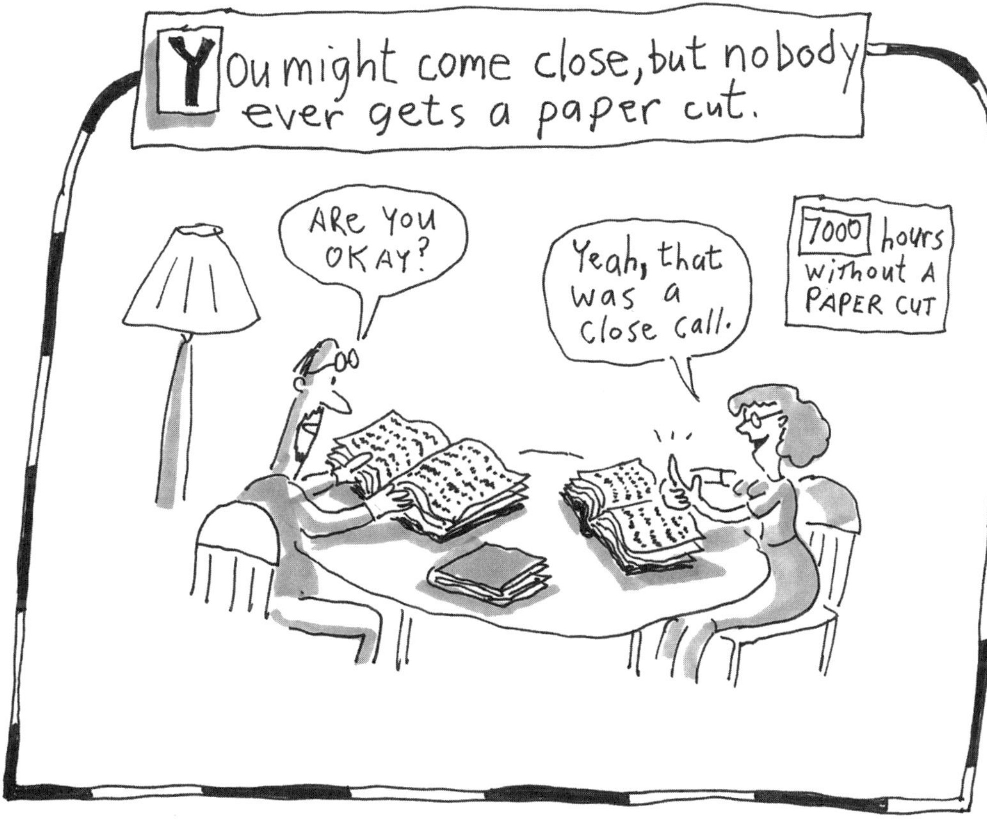
You might come close, but nobody ever gets a paper cut.
ARE YOU OKAY?
Yeah, that was a close call.
7000 hours without A PAPER CUT

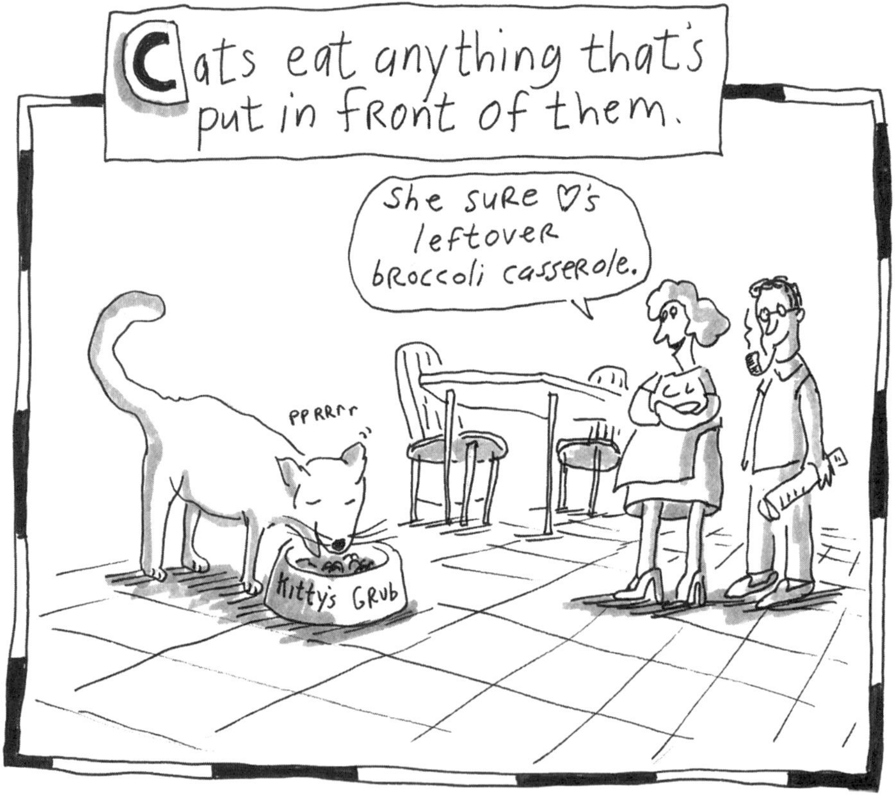
Cats eat anything that's put in front of them.
She sure ♡'s leftover broccoli casserole.
PPRRrr
Kitty's GRub

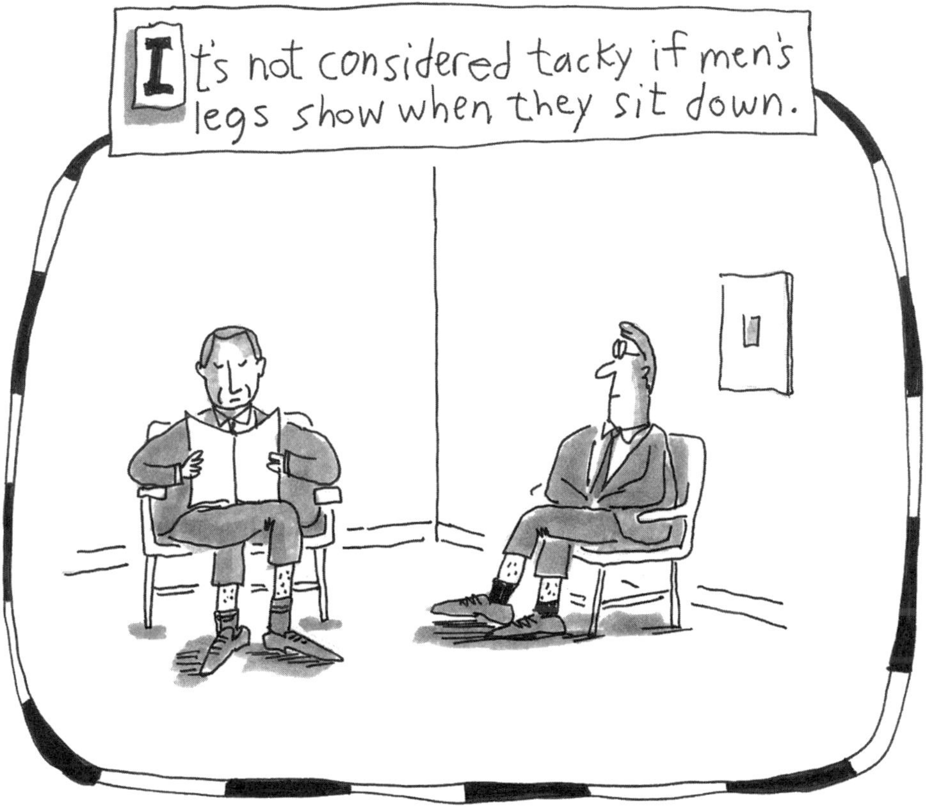
It's not considered tacky if men's legs show when they sit down.

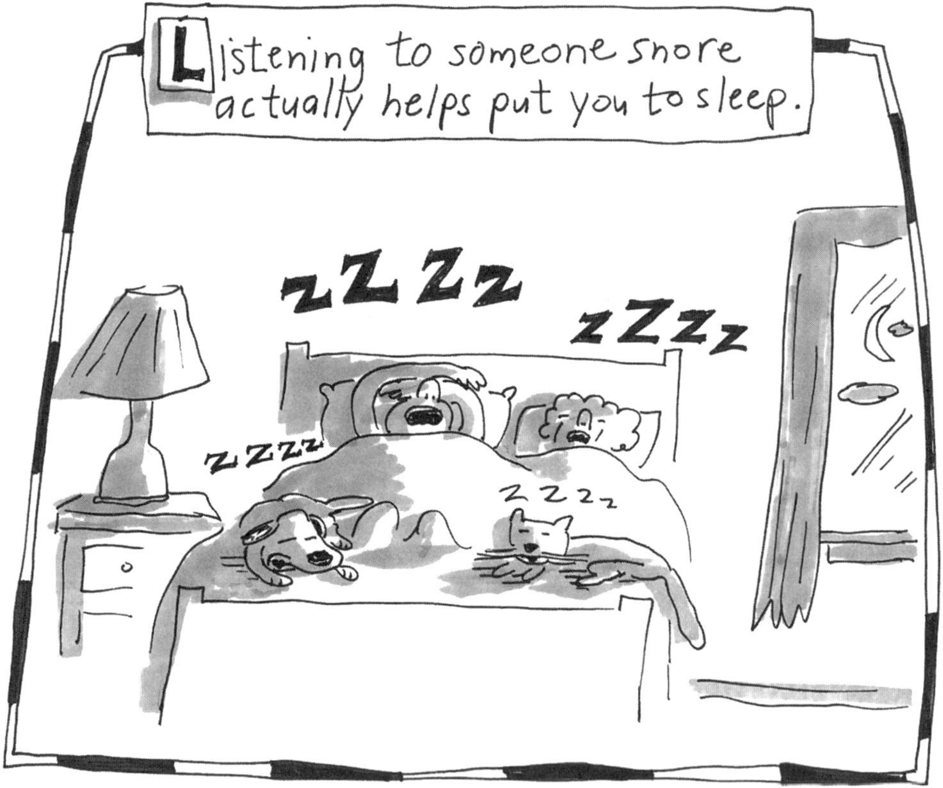
Listening to someone snore actually helps put you to sleep.
zZZZz
zZZzz
zzzzz
ZZzz

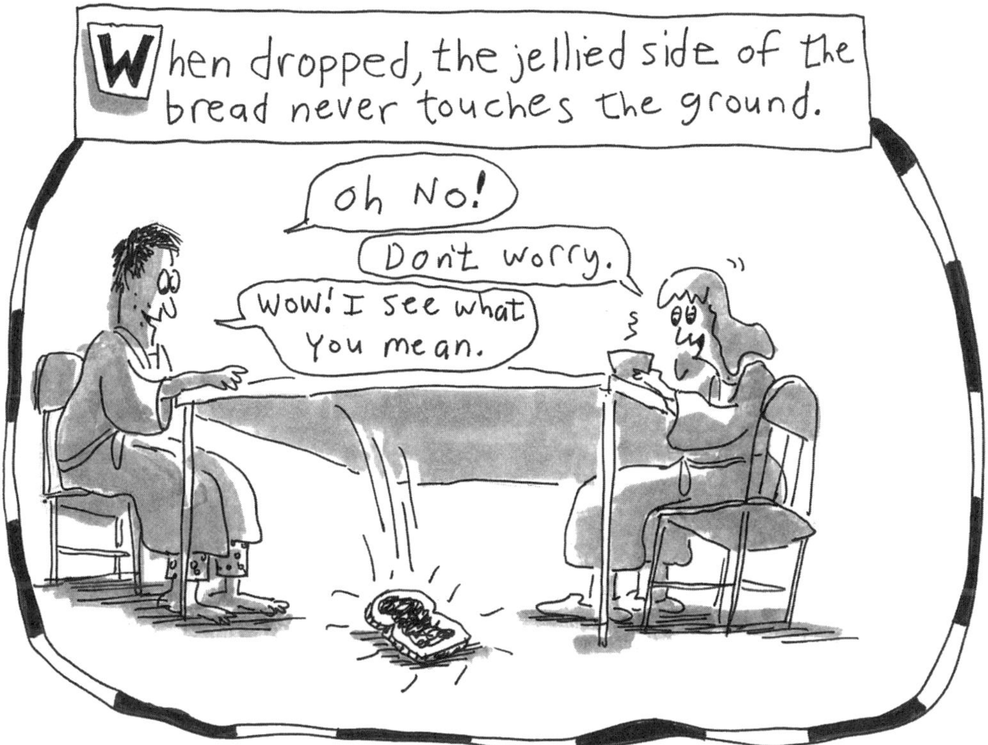
When dropped, the jellied side of the bread never touches the ground.
Oh No!
Don't worry.
Wow! I see what you mean.

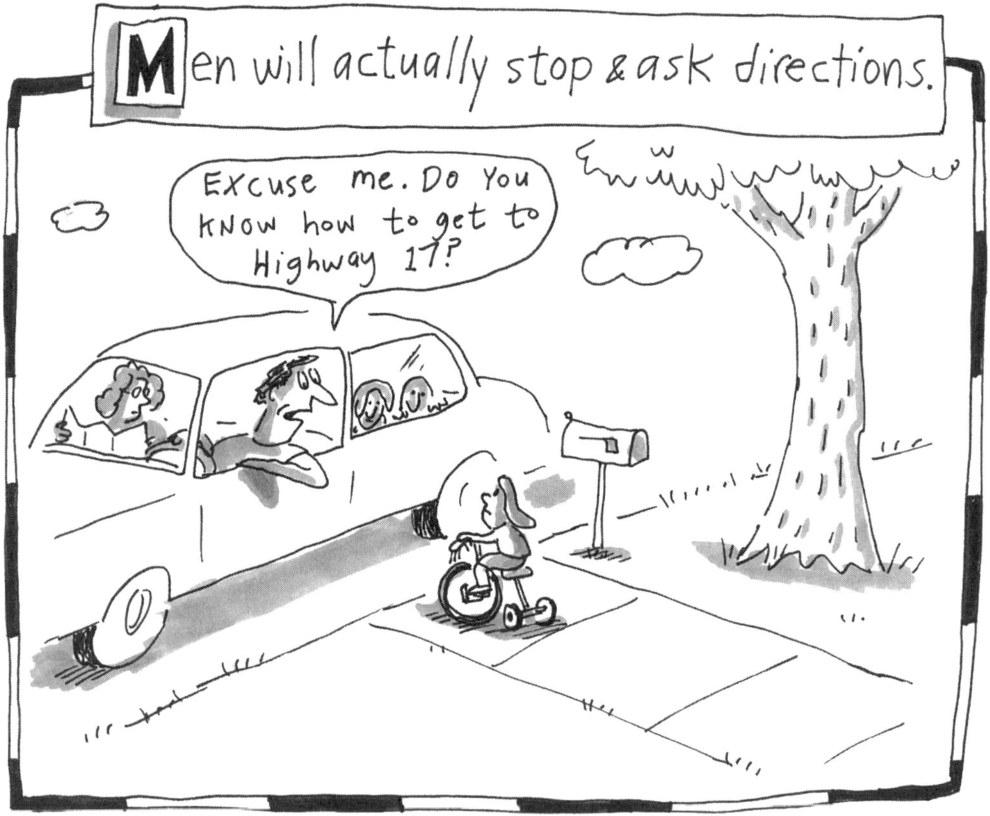
Men will actually stop & ask directions.
Excuse me. Do you know how to get to Highway 17?

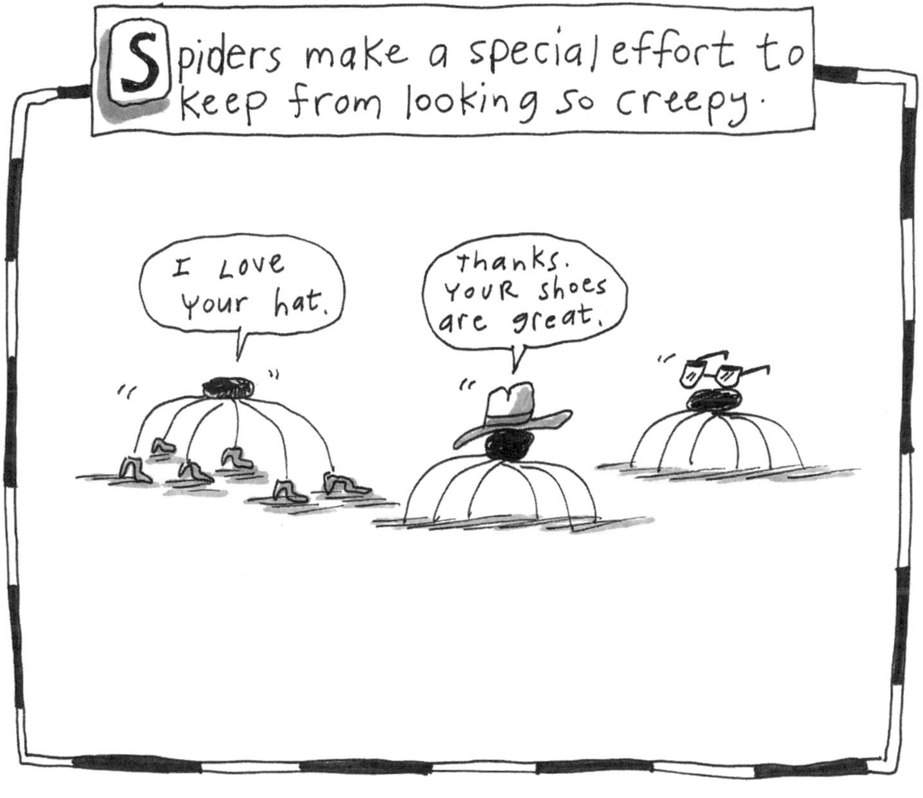
Spiders make a special effort to keep from looking so creepy.
I LOVE your hat.
Thanks. YOUR shoes are great.

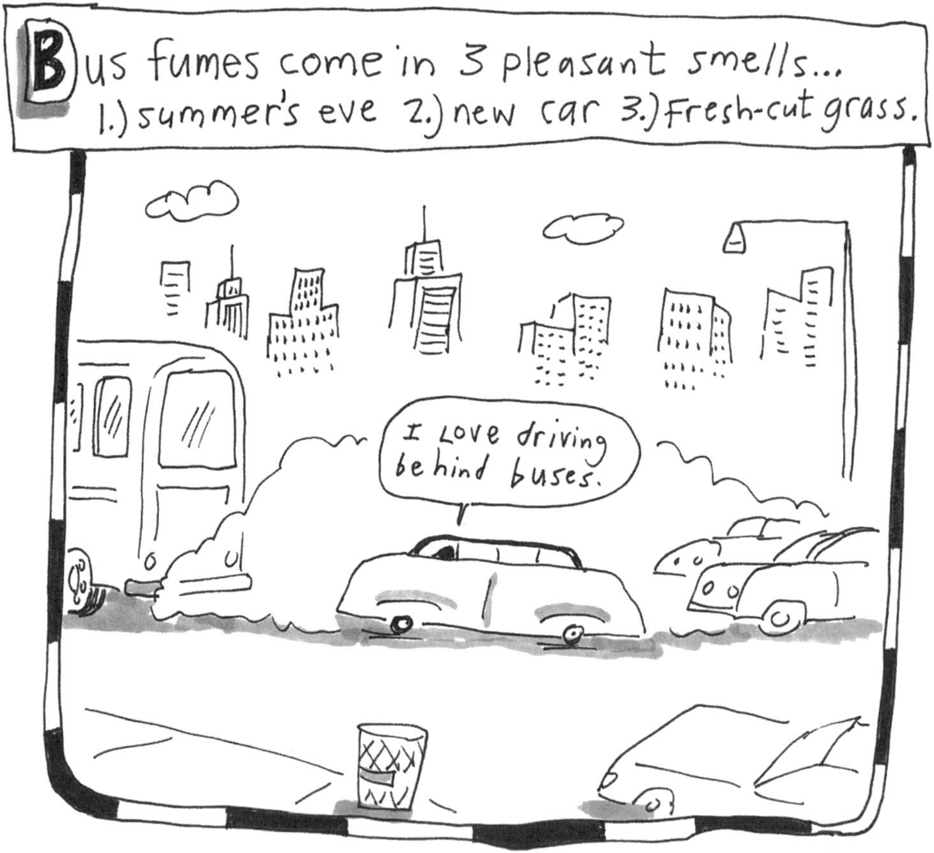
Bus fumes come in 3 pleasant smells...
1.) summer's eve 2.) new car 3.) Fresh-cut grass.
I Love driving behind buses.

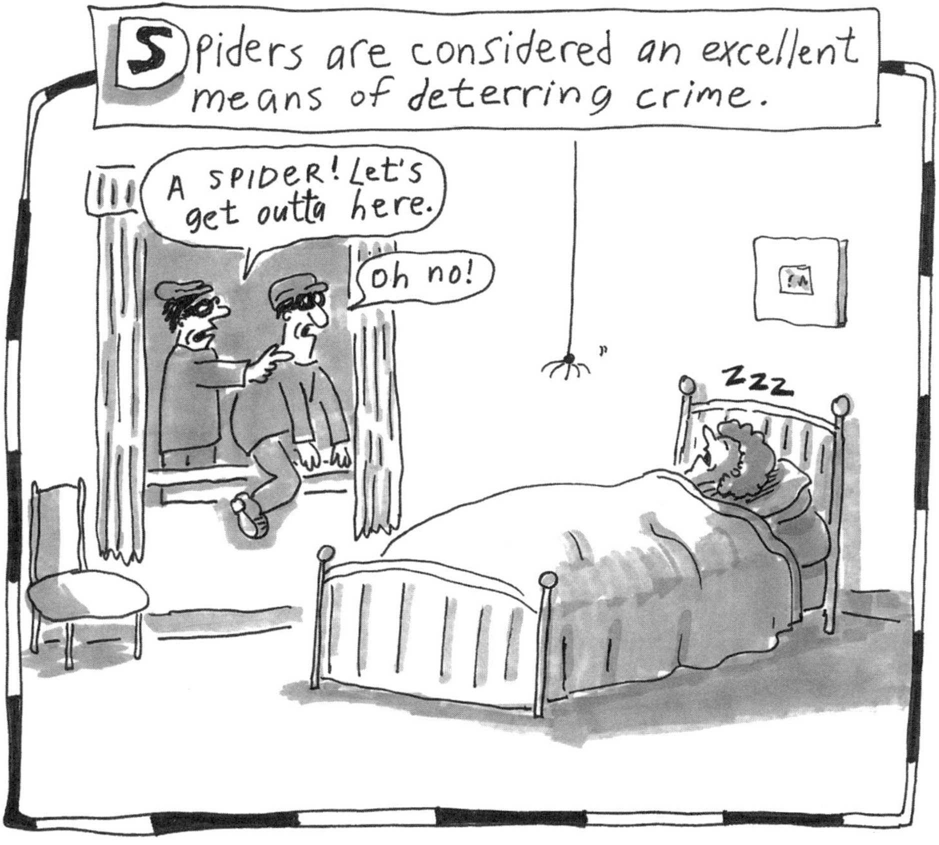
Spiders are considered an excellent means of deterring crime.
A SPIDER! Let's get outta here.
Oh no!
ZZZ

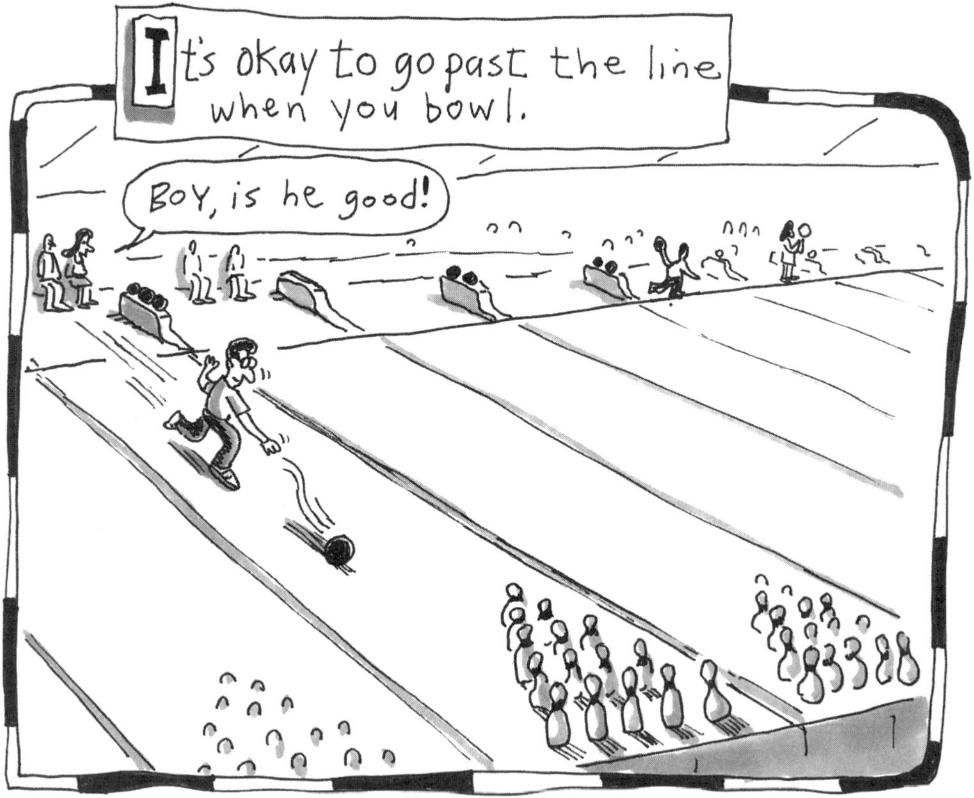
It's okay to go past the line when you bowl.
Boy, is he good!

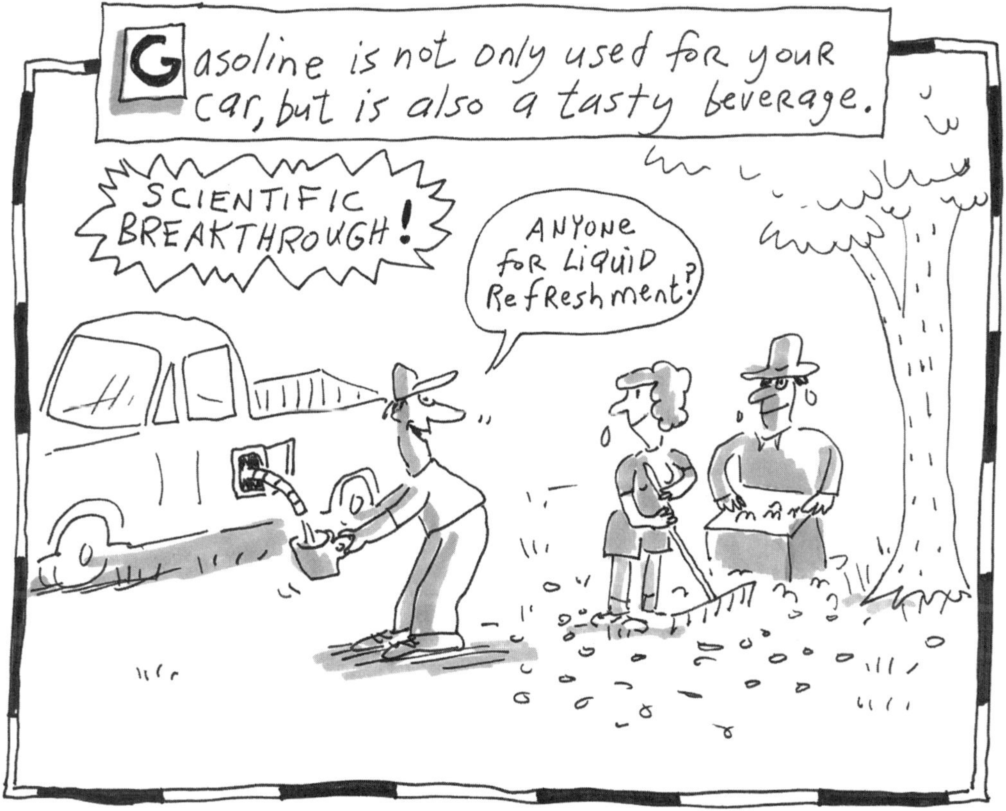
Gasoline is not only used for your car, but is also a tasty beverage.
SCIENTIFIC BREAKTHROUGH!
ANYONE for LIQUID Refreshment?

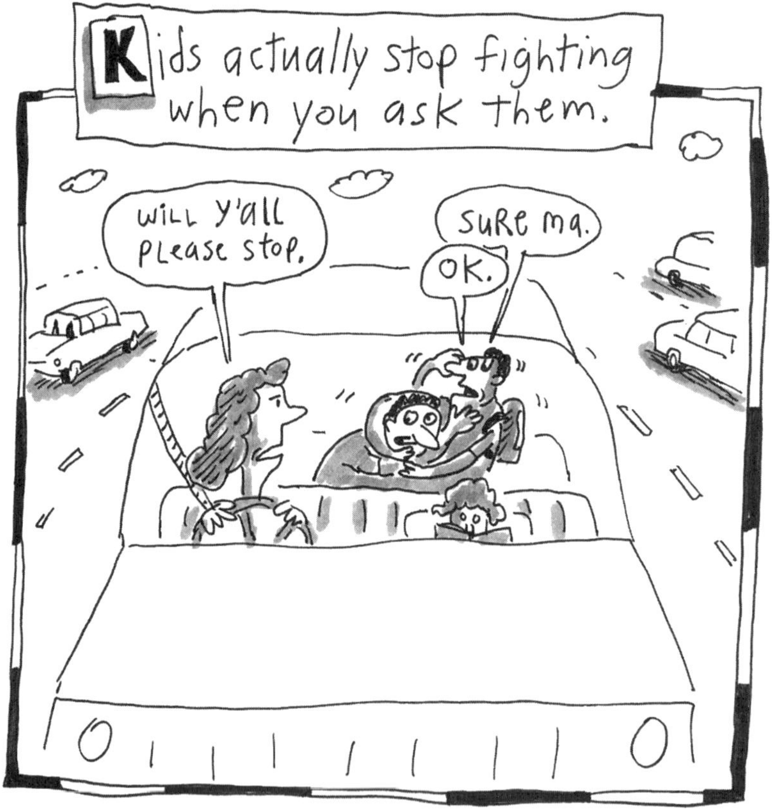
Kids actually stop fighting when you ask them.
WILL Y'ALL PLEASE STOP.
SURE MA.
OK.

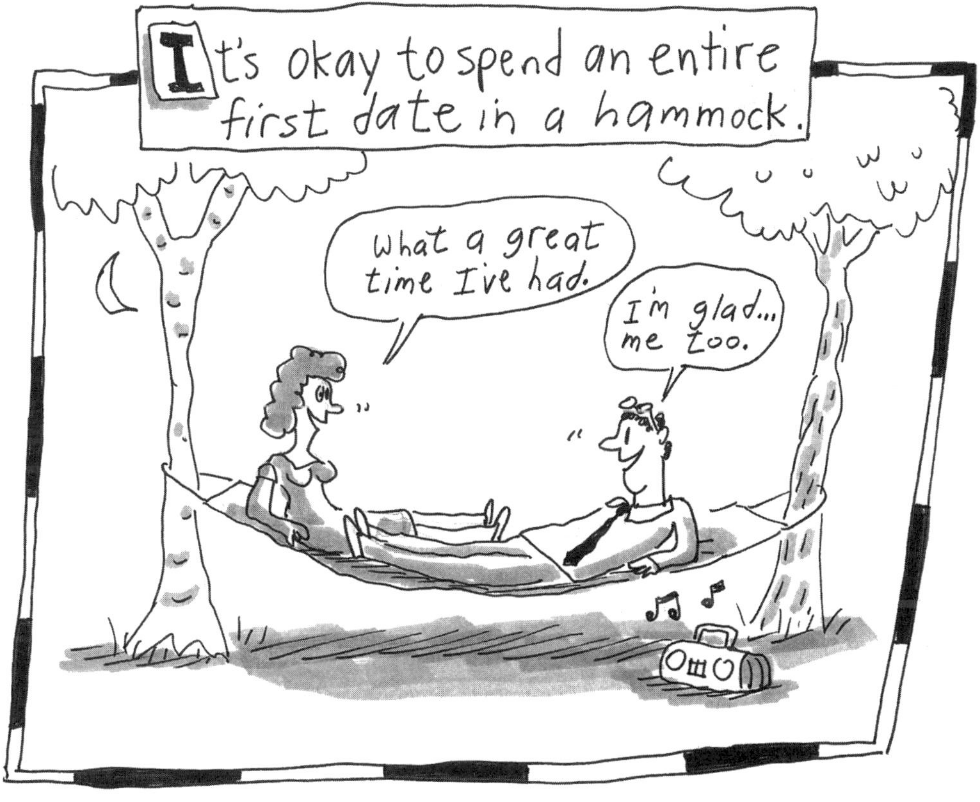
It's okay to spend an entire first date in a hammock.
What a great time I've had.
I'm glad... me too.

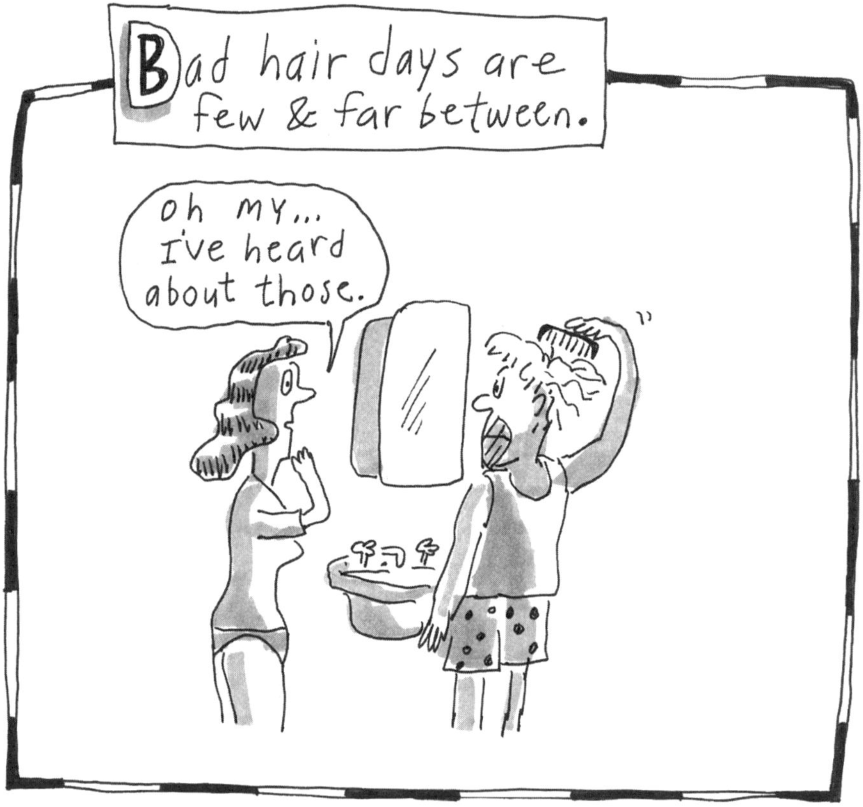
Bad hair days are few & far between.
oh my... I've heard about those.

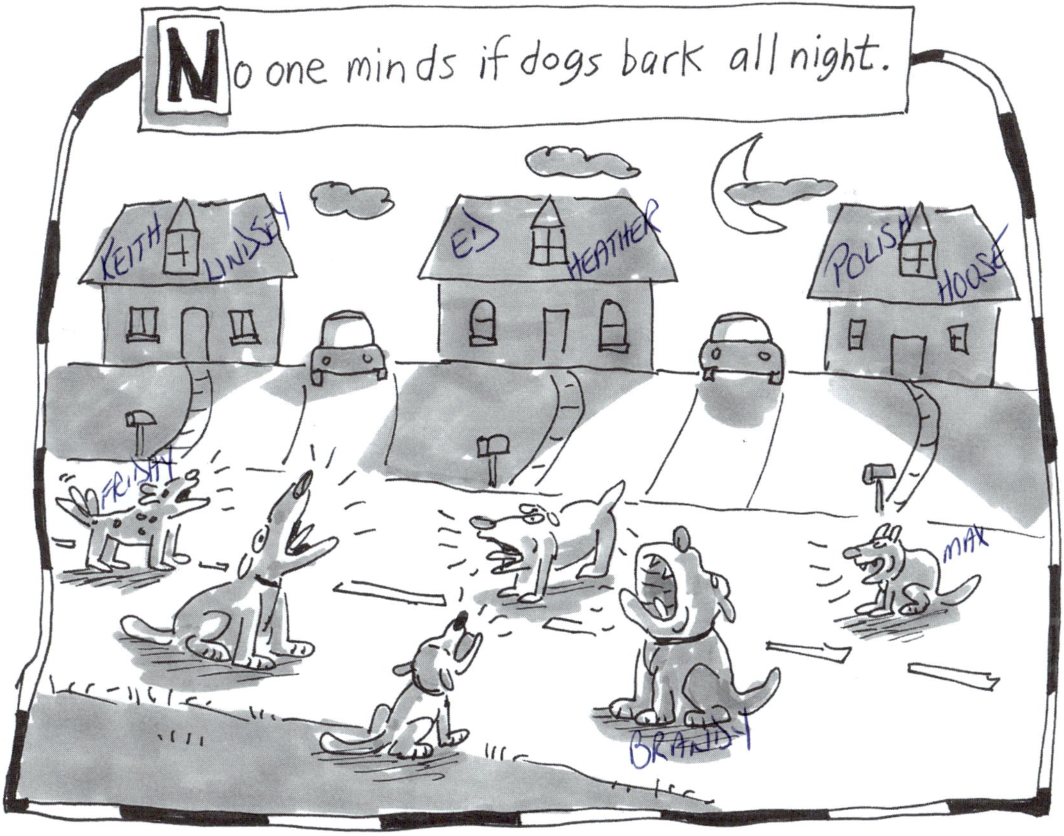
No one minds if dogs bark all night.
KEITH
LINDSEY
EJ
HEATHER
POLISH
HOUSE
FRIDAY
MAX
BRANDY

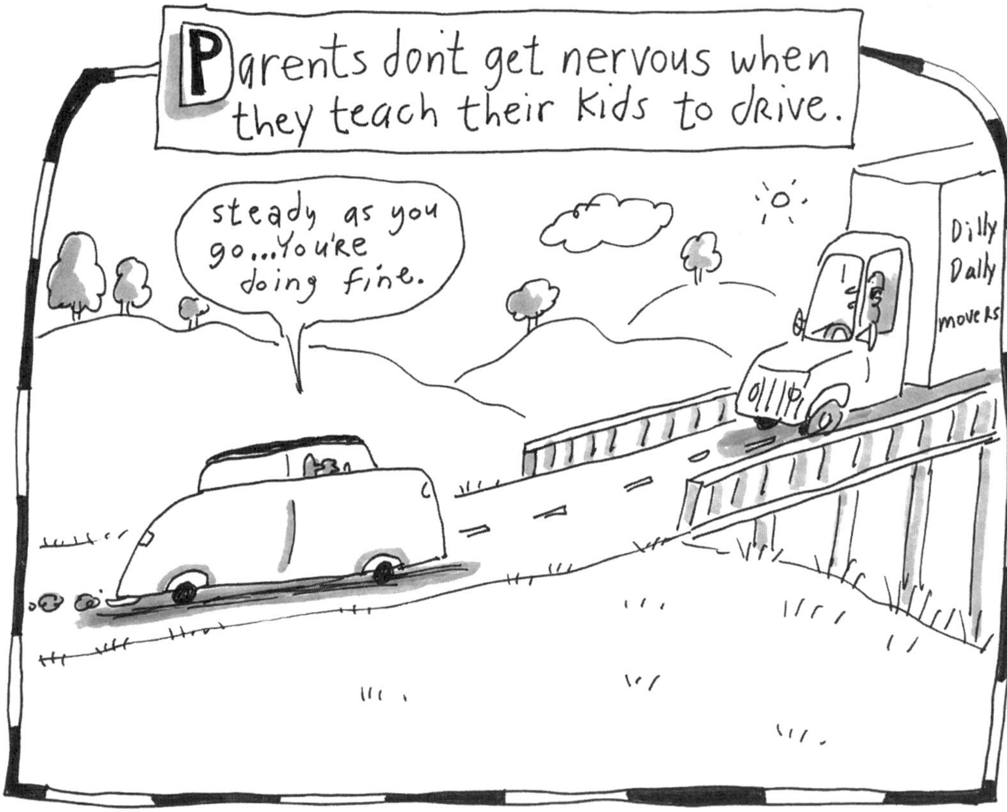
Parents don't get nervous when they teach their kids to drive.
steady as you go...You're doing fine.
Dilly Dally movers

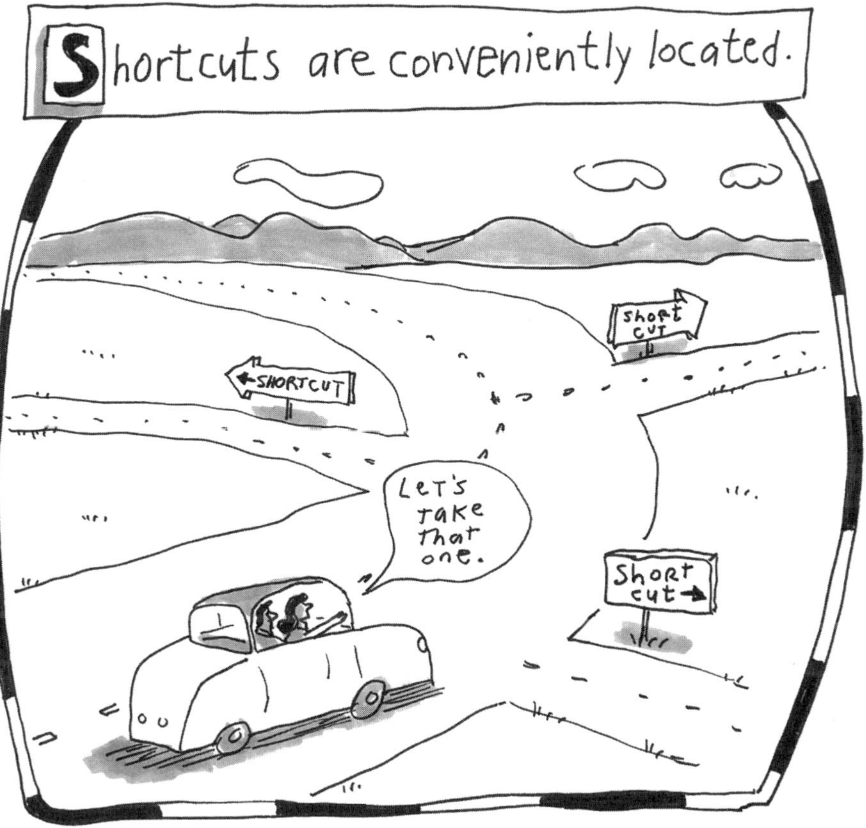
Shortcuts are conveniently located.
SHORT CUT
←SHORTCUT
LET'S TAKE THAT ONE.
Short cut→

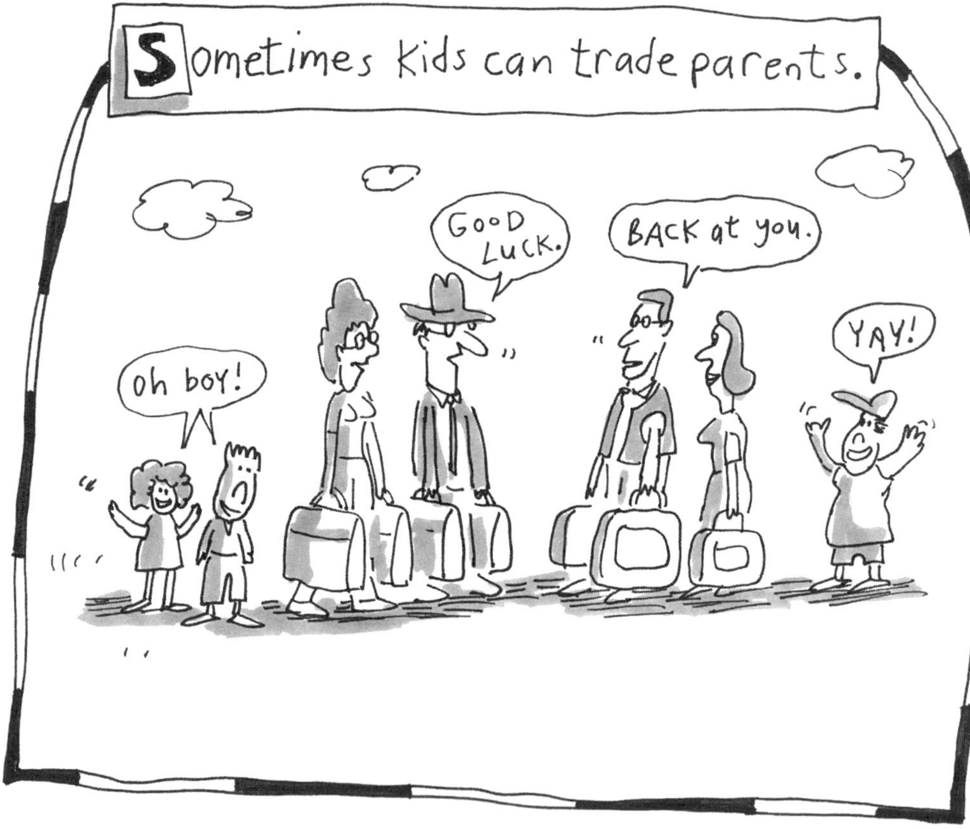
Oh boy!
GOOD LUCK.
BACK at you.
YAY!

Sometimes kids can trade parents.

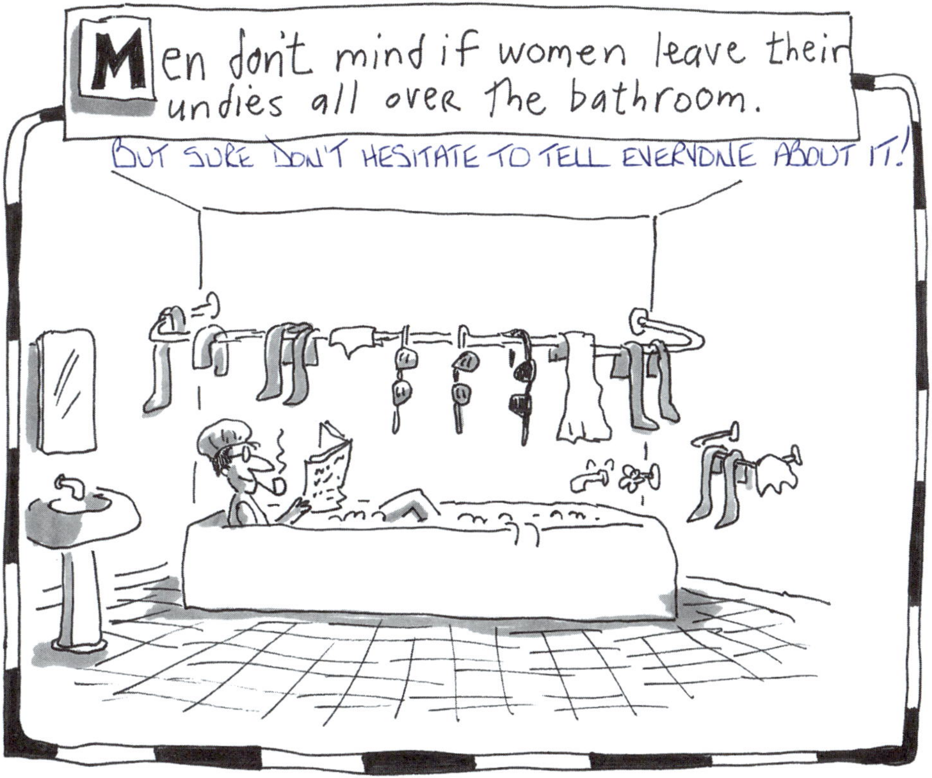

Men don't mind if women leave their undies all over the bathroom.
BUT SURE DON'T HESITATE TO TELL EVERYONE ABOUT IT!

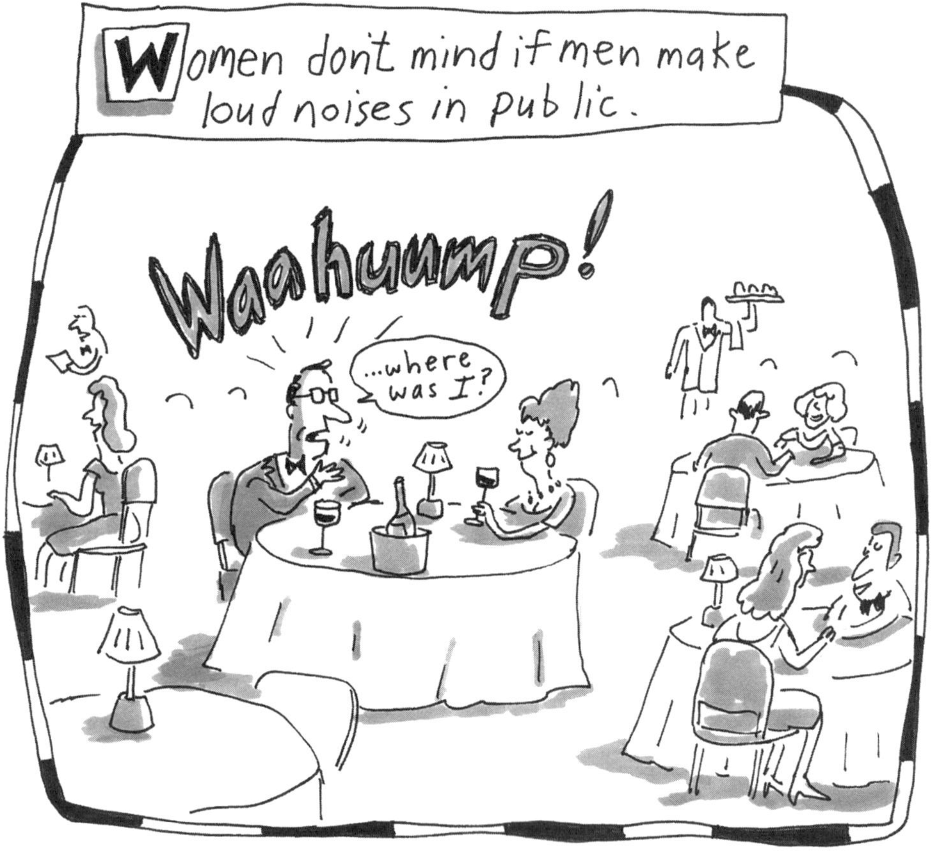
Women don't mind if men make loud noises in public.
Waahuump!
...where was I?

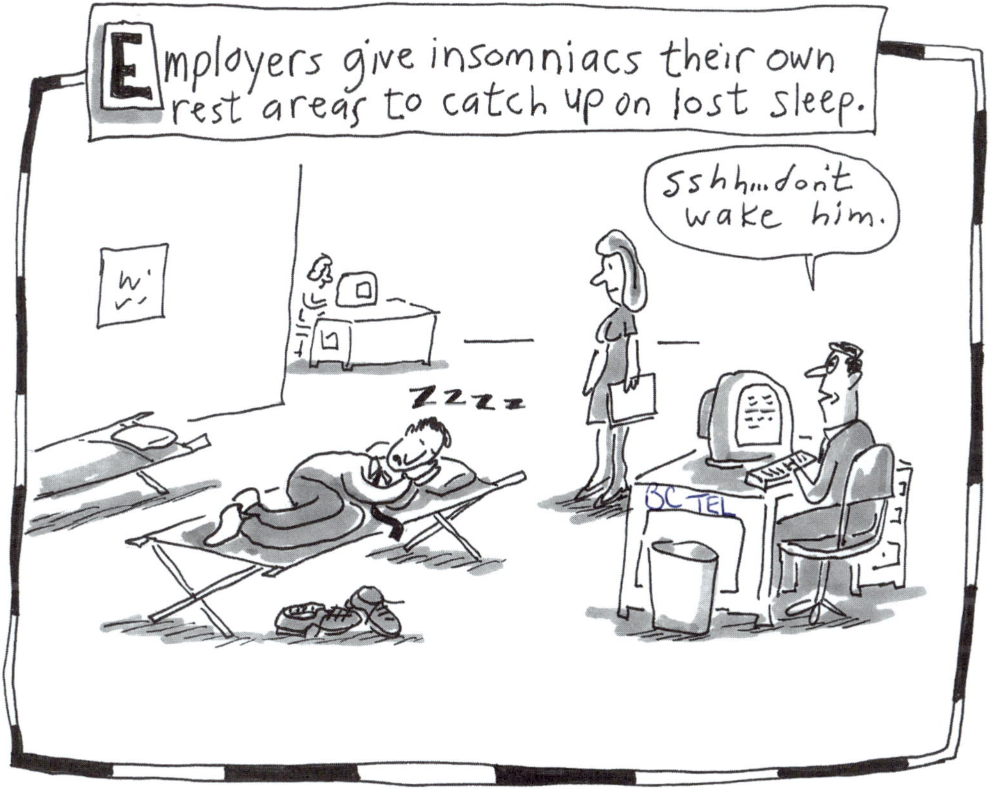
Employers give insomniacs their own rest areas to catch up on lost sleep.
sshh...don't wake him.
ZZZZ
BC TEL

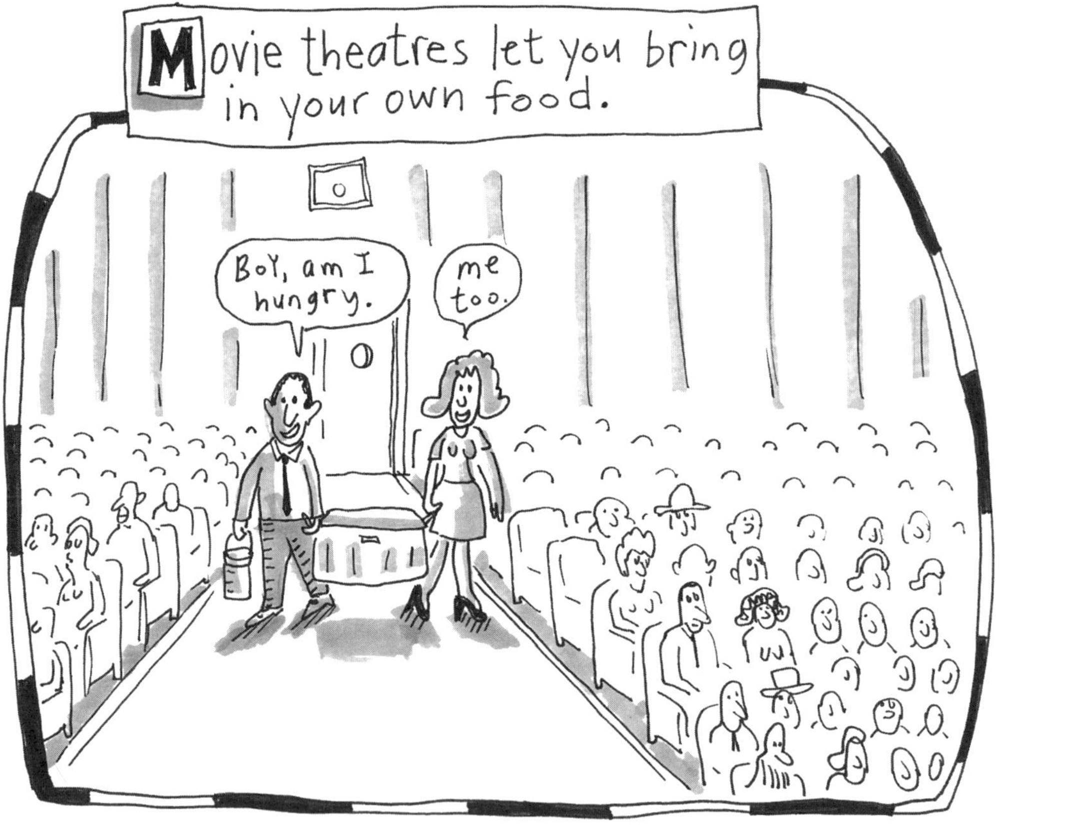
Movie theatres let you bring in your own food.
Boy, am I hungry.
me too.

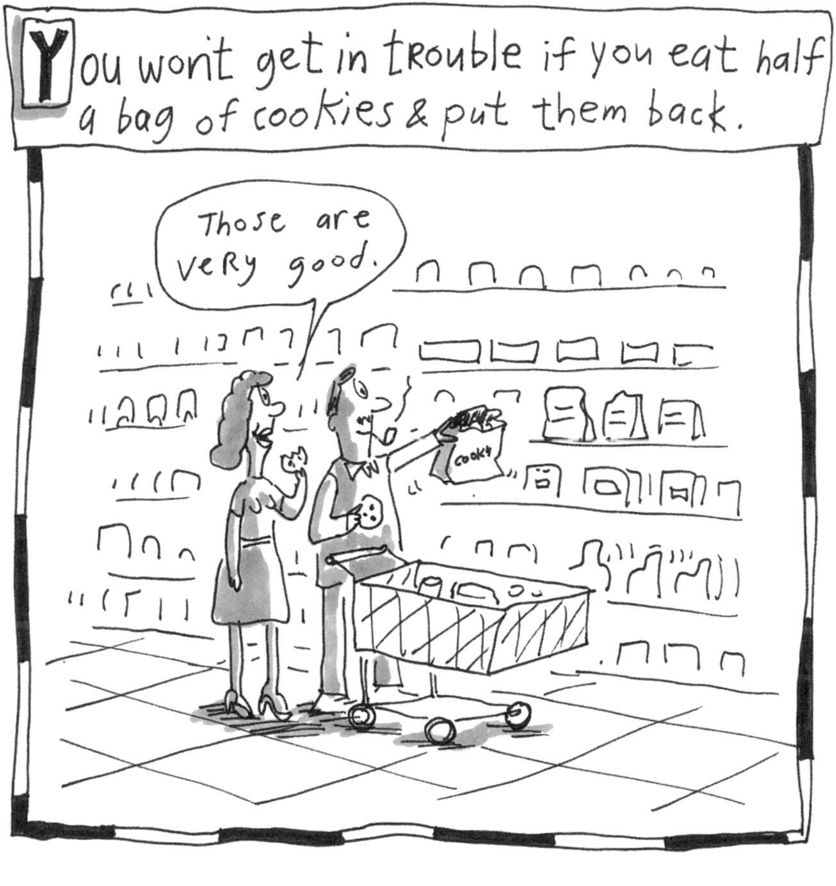
You won't get in trouble if you eat half a bag of cookies & put them back.
Those are very good.

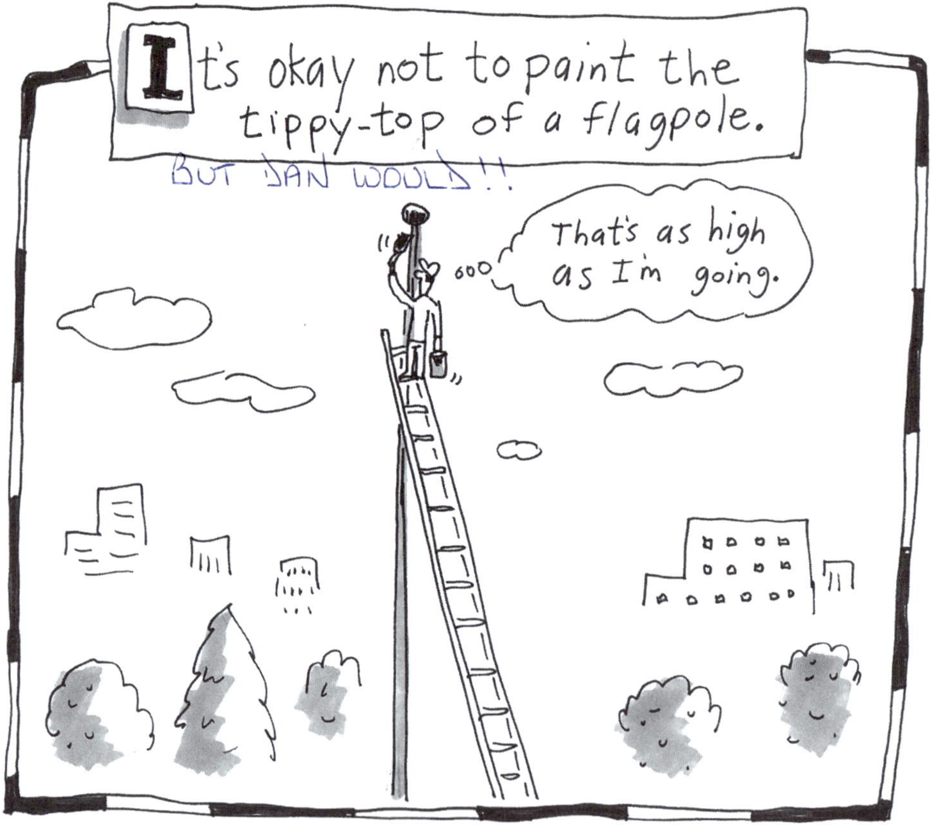
It's okay not to paint the tippy-top of a flagpole.
BUT DAN WOULD!!
That's as high as I'm going.

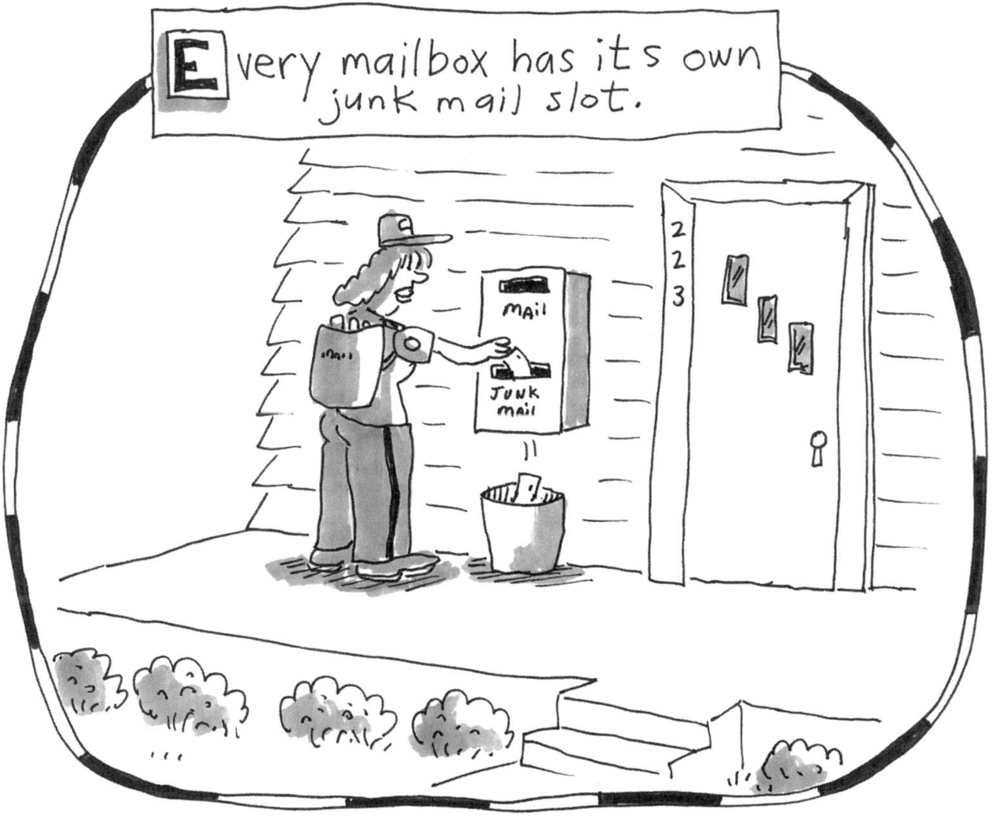
Every mailbox has its own junk mail slot.
MAIL
JUNK mail
2 2 3

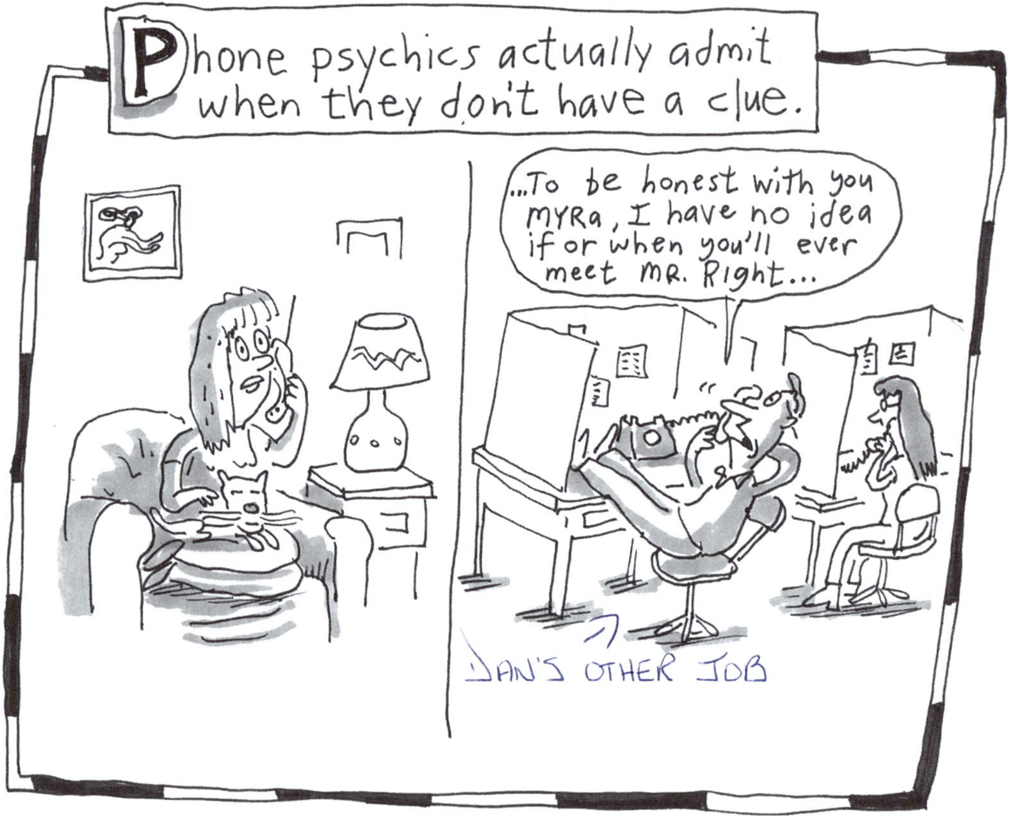
Phone psychics actually admit when they don't have a clue.
...To be honest with you MYRA, I have no idea if or when you'll ever meet MR. Right...
DAN'S OTHER JOB

Losing change in a snack machine means you can claim it as your own.

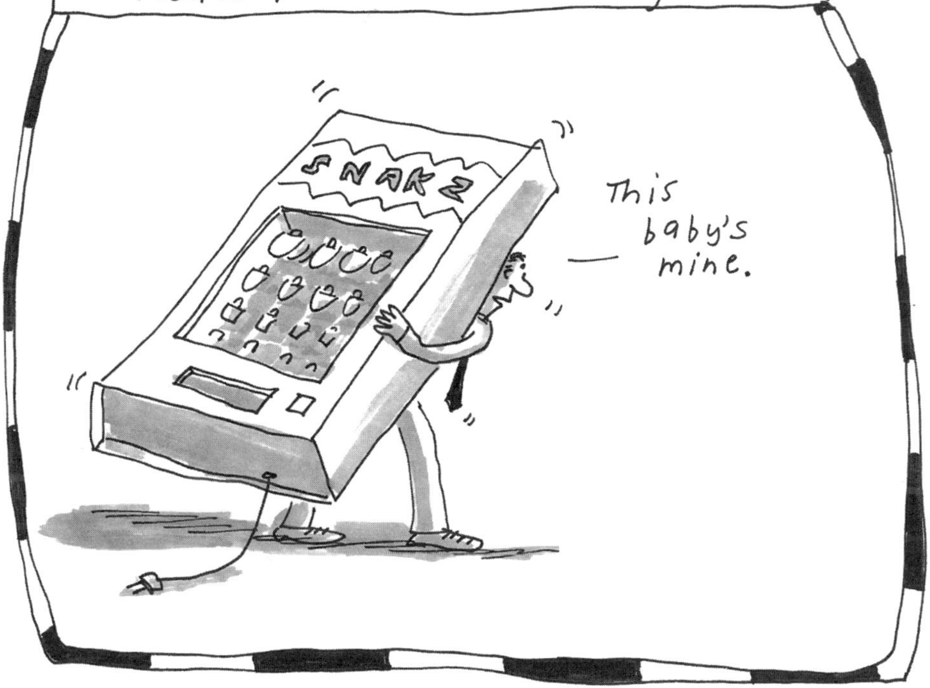
SNAKZ
This baby's mine.

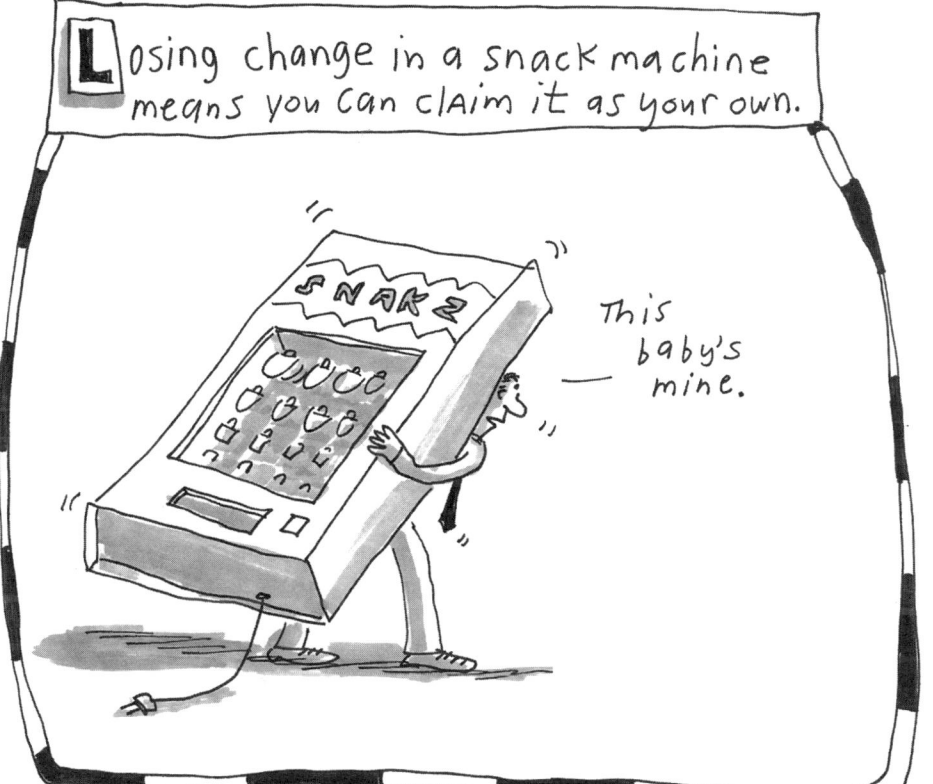

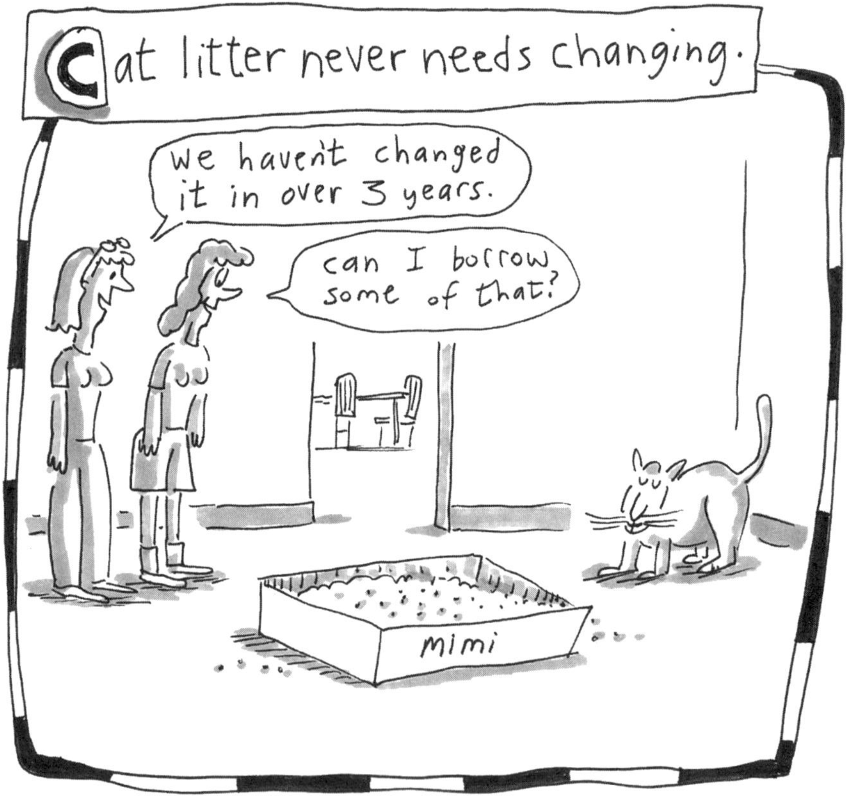
Cat litter never needs changing.
we haven't changed it in over 3 years.
can I borrow some of that?
mimi

76

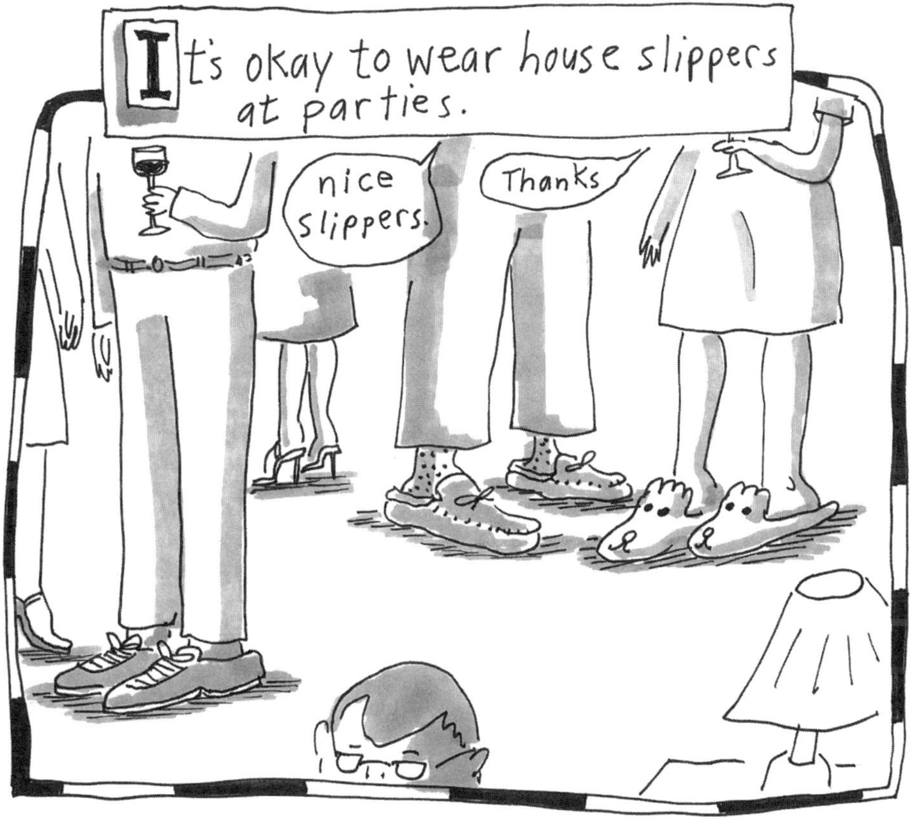
It's okay to wear house slippers at parties.
nice slippers.
Thanks

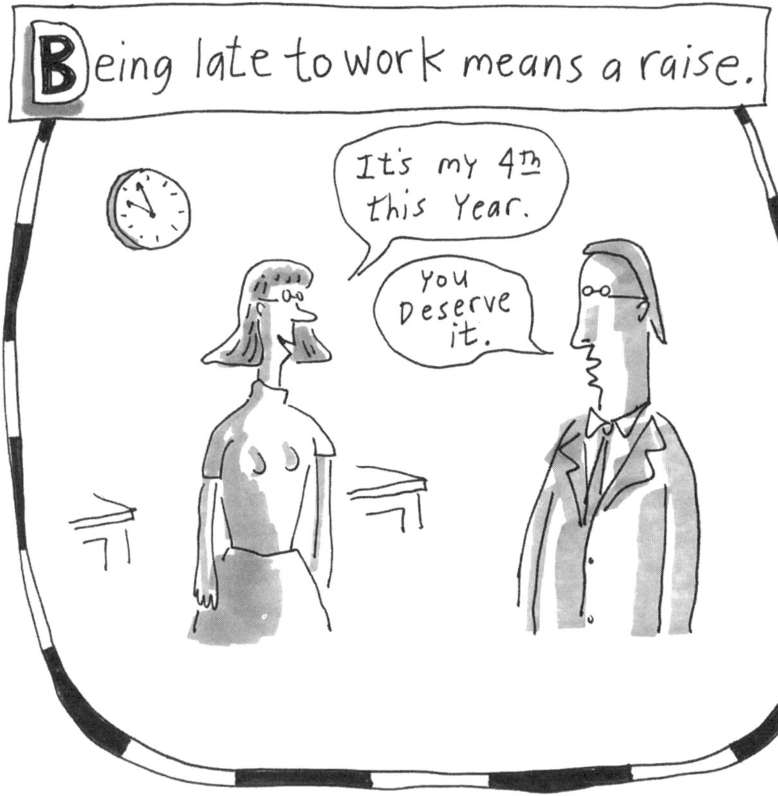
Being late to work means a raise.
It's my 4th this Year.
You Deserve it.

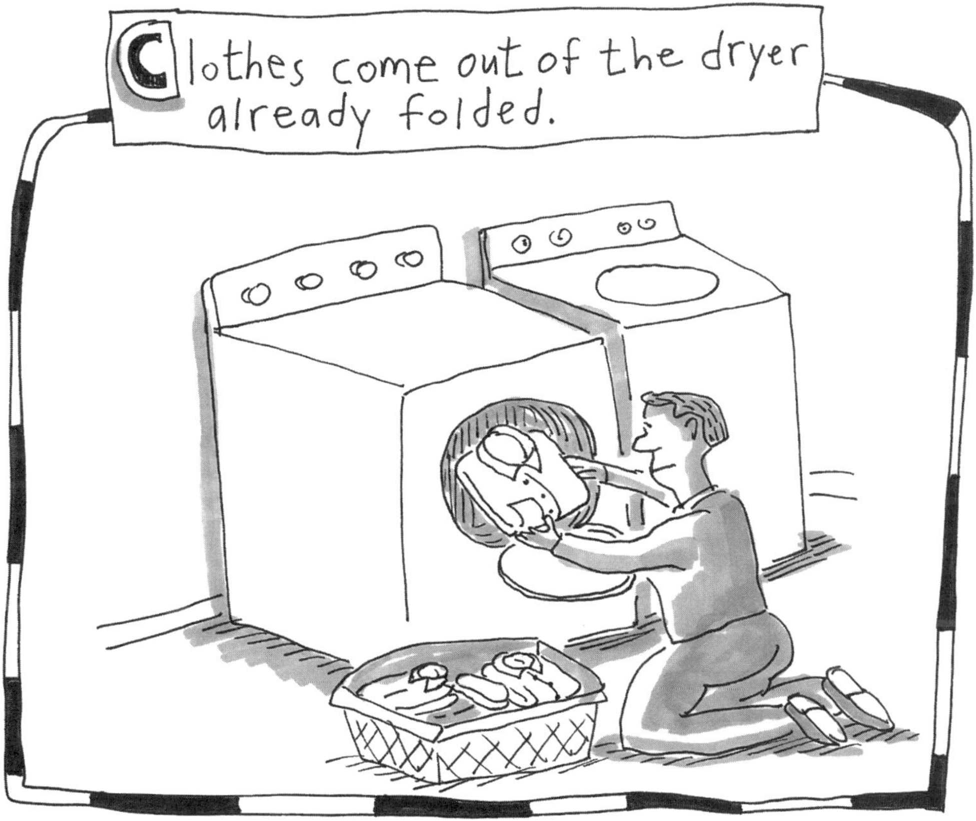
Clothes come out of the dryer already folded.

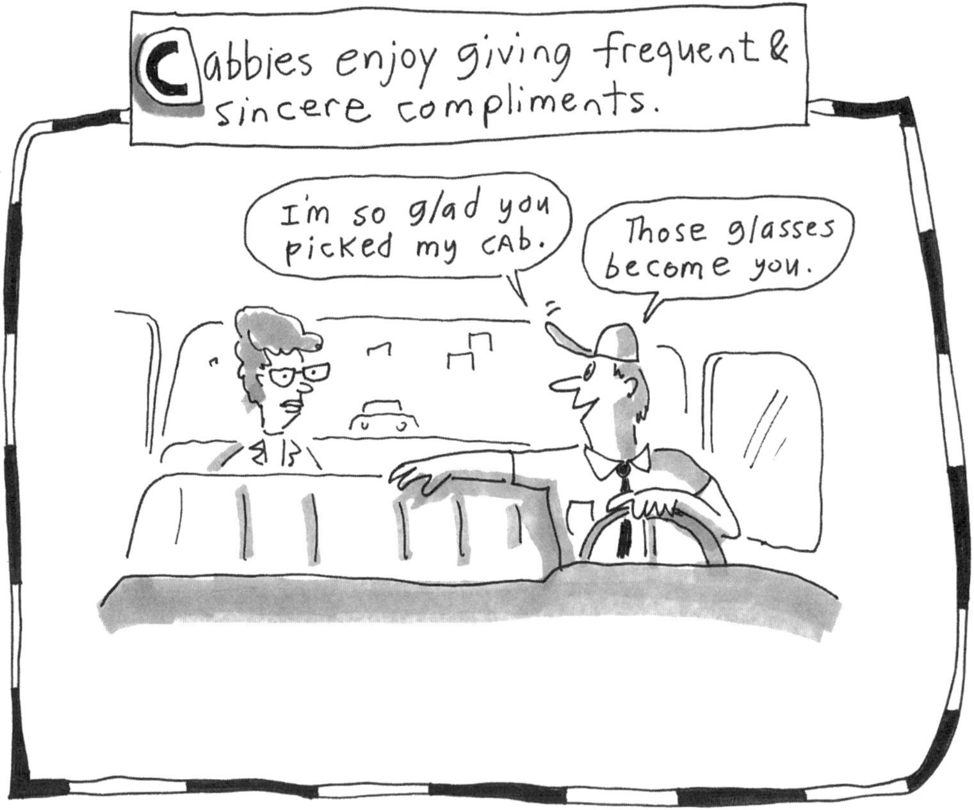
Cabbies enjoy giving frequent & sincere compliments.
I'm so glad you picked my cab.
Those glasses become you.

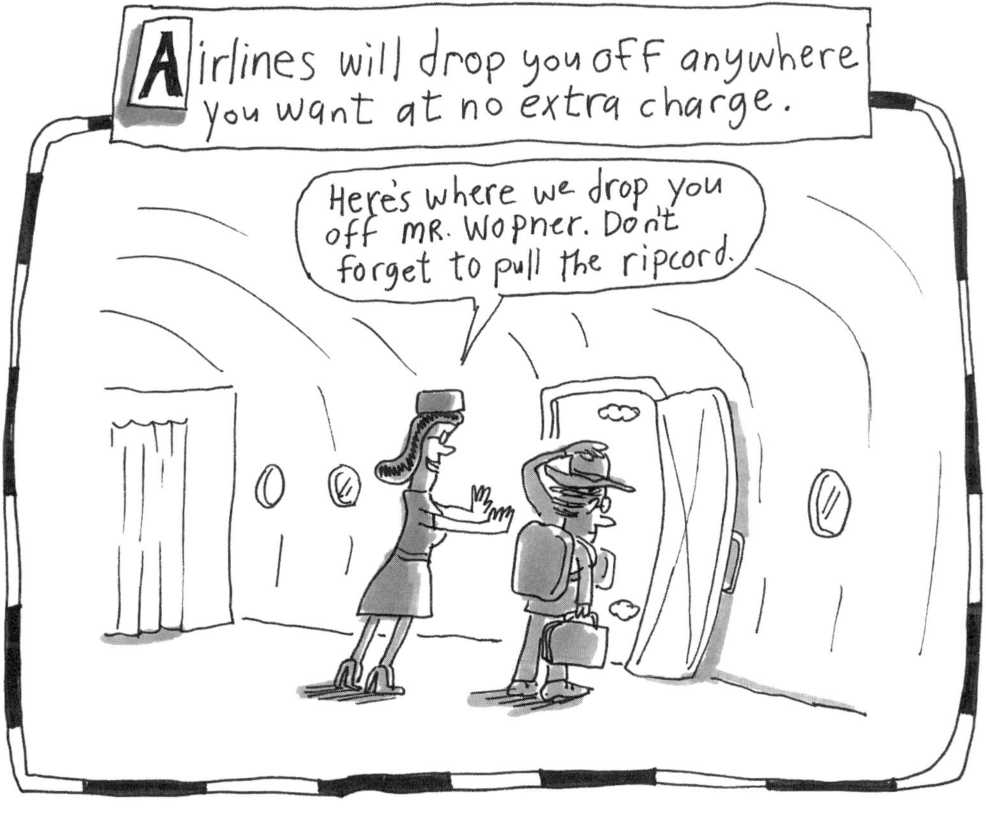
Airlines will drop you off anywhere you want at no extra charge.
Here's where we drop you off MR. Wopner. Don't forget to pull the ripcord.

Many kids ride a roller coaster to and from school.

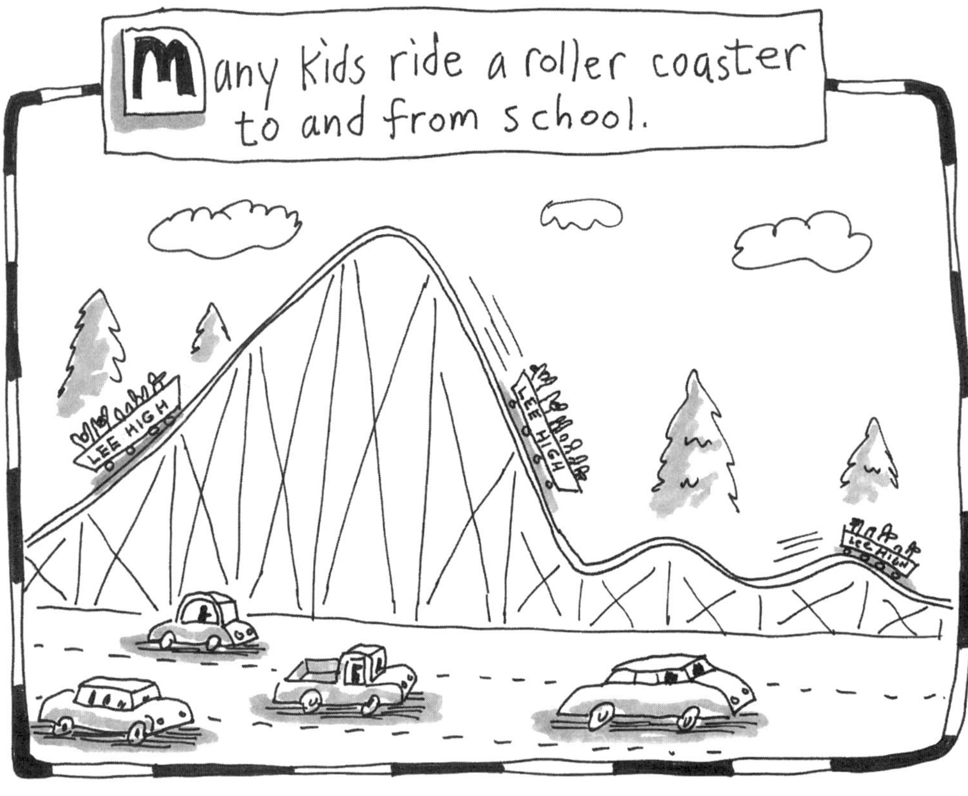
LEE HIGH
LEE HIGH
LEE HIGH

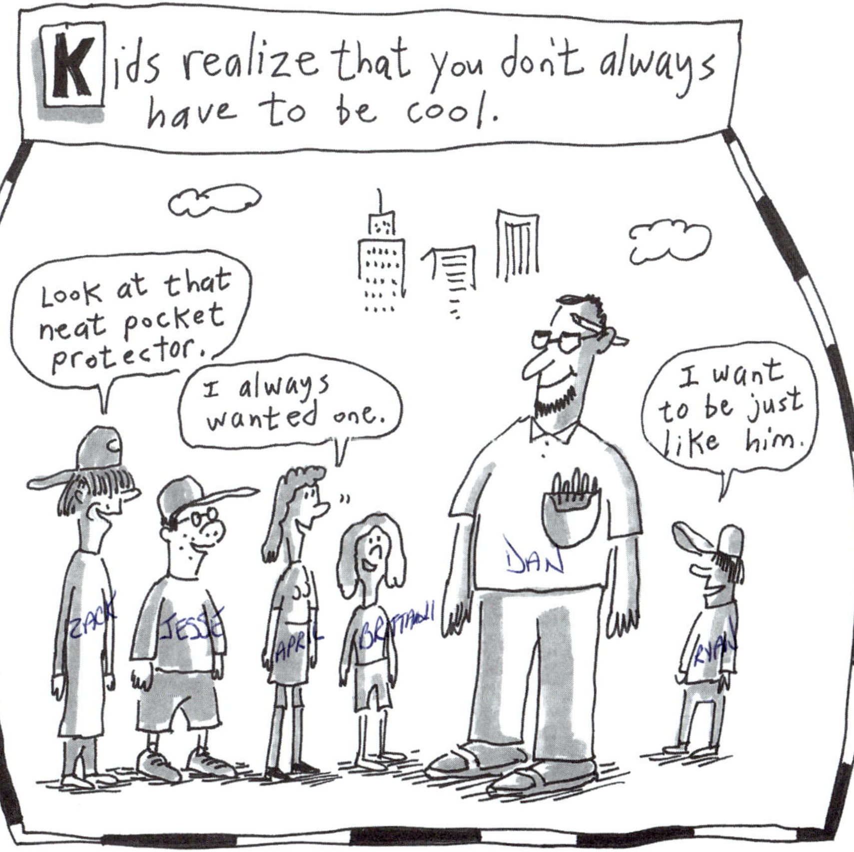
Kids realize that you don't always have to be cool.
Look at that neat pocket protector.
I always wanted one.
I want to be just like him.

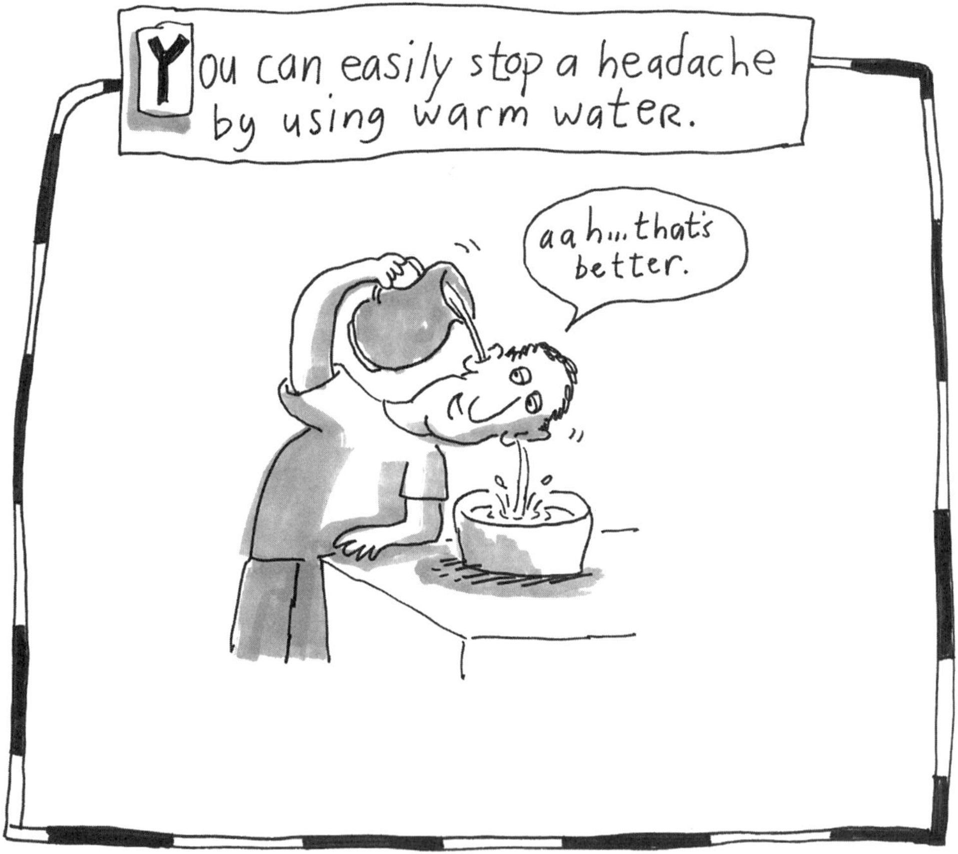
You can easily stop a headache by using warm water.
aah... that's better.

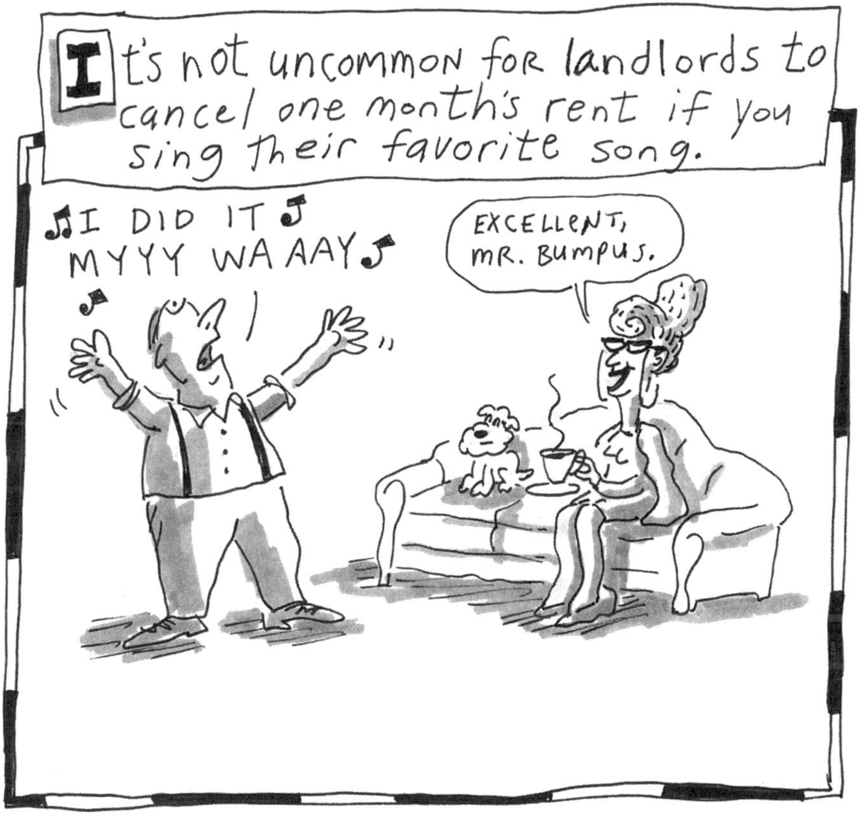
It's not uncommon for landlords to cancel one month's rent if you sing their favorite song.
I DID IT MYYY WAAAY
EXCELLENT, MR. BUMPUS.

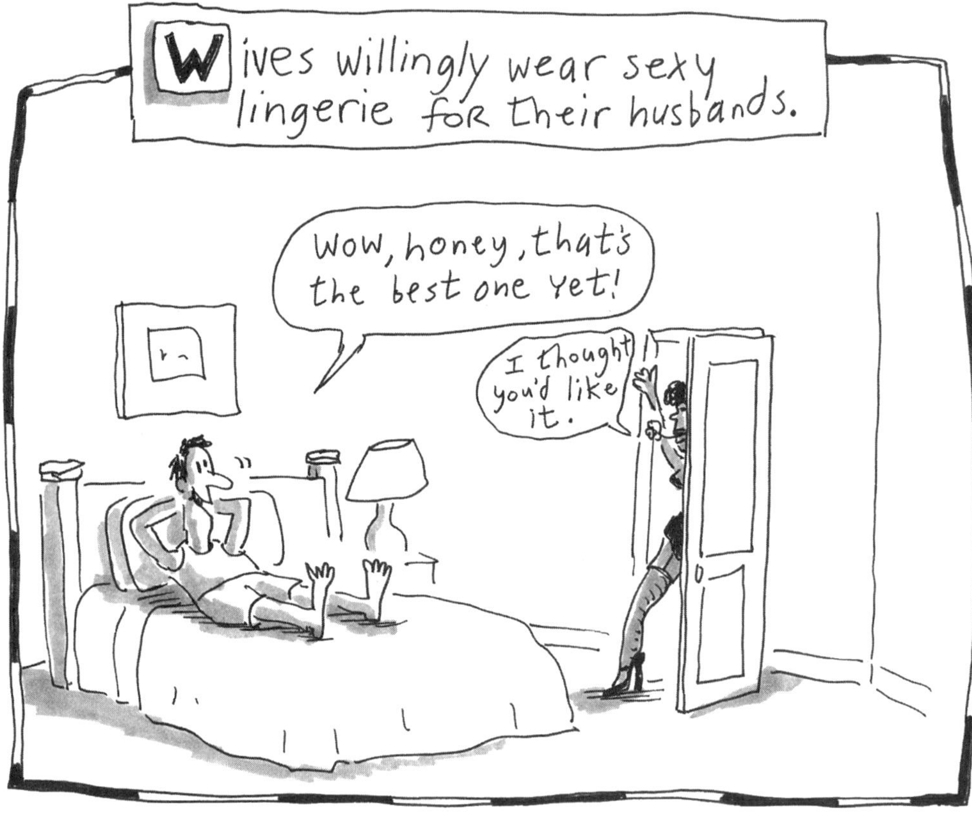
Wives willingly wear sexy lingerie for their husbands.
Wow, honey, that's the best one yet!
I thought you'd like it.

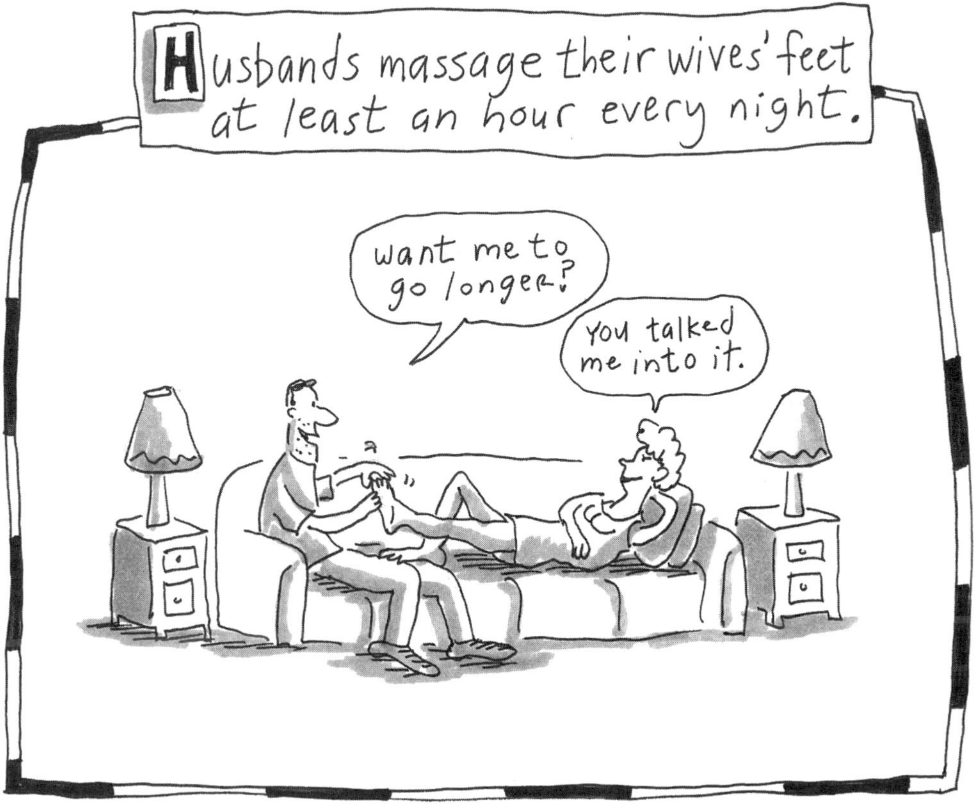
Husbands massage their wives' feet at least an hour every night.
want me to go longer?
You talked me into it.

87

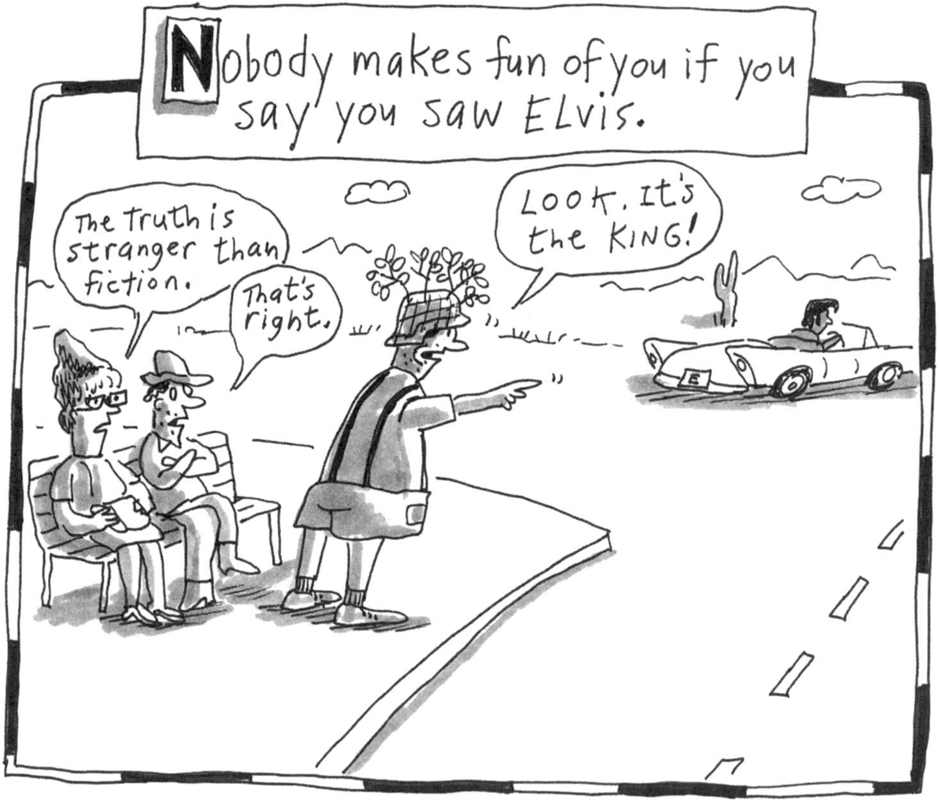

Nobody makes fun of you if you say you saw Elvis.
The truth is stranger than fiction.
That's right.
LOOK. It's the KING!
E

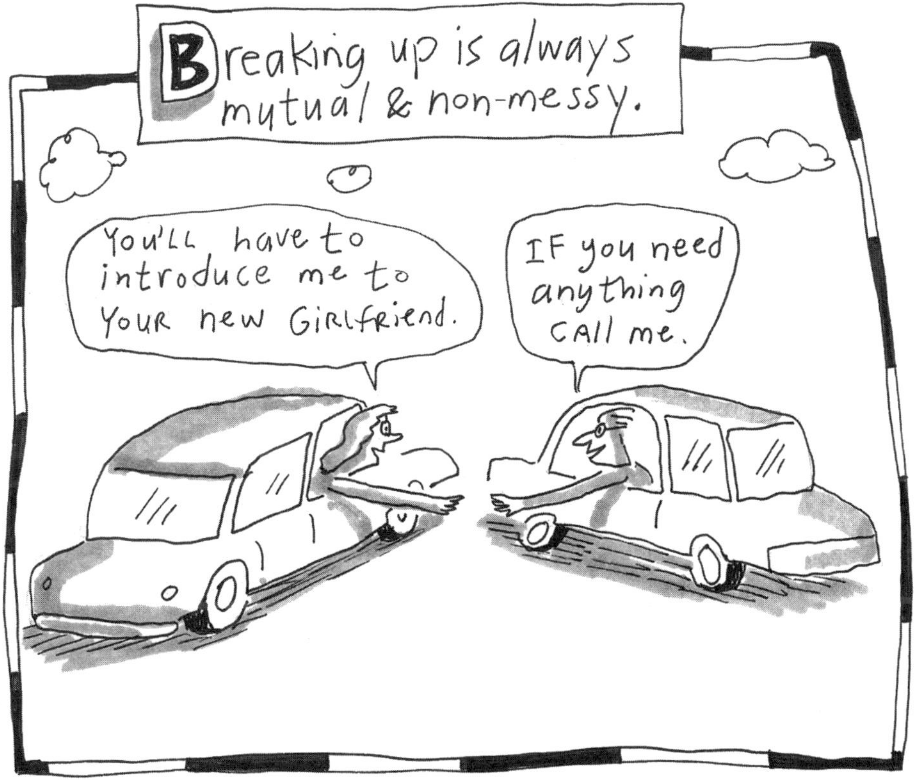
Breaking up is always mutual & non-messy.
You'll have to introduce me to your new girlfriend.
If you need anything call me.

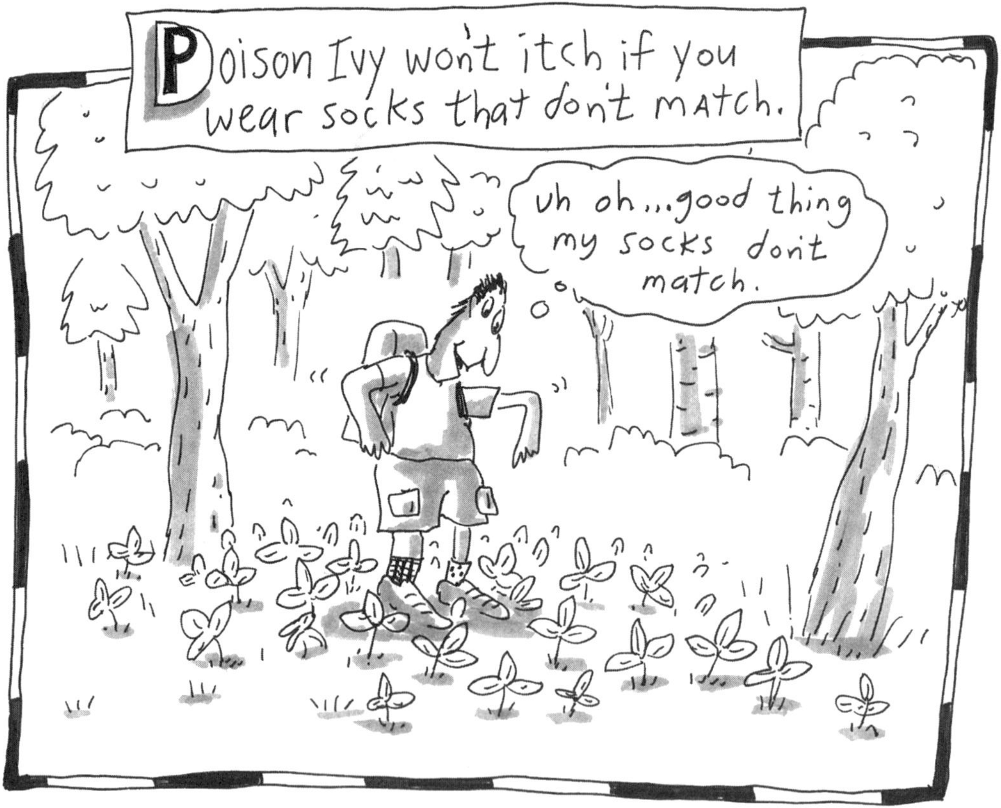
Poison Ivy won't itch if you wear socks that don't match.
uh oh...good thing my socks don't match.

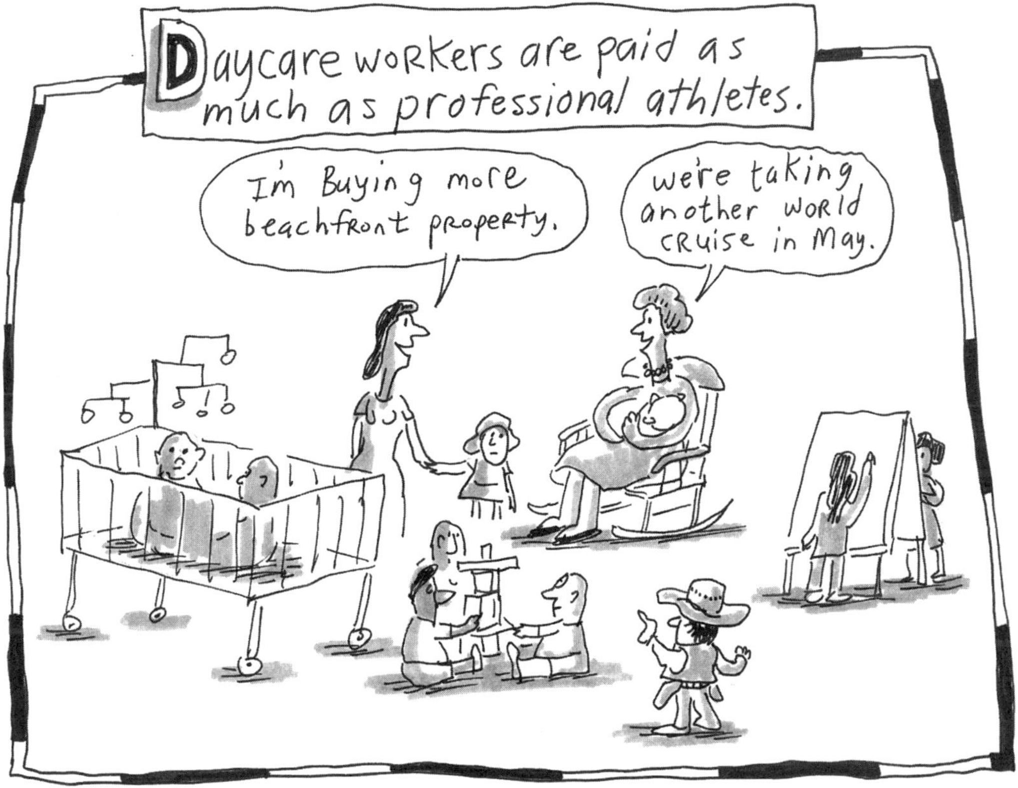
Daycare workers are paid as much as professional athletes.
I'm Buying more beachfront property.
we're taking another world cruise in May.

92

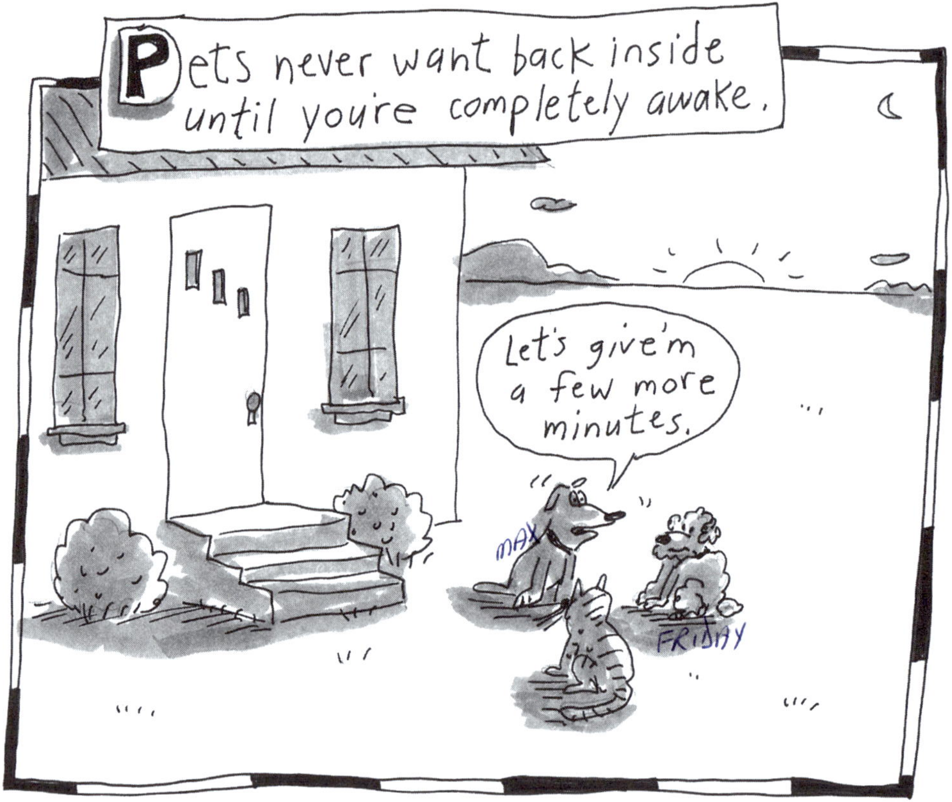
Pets never want back inside until you're completely awake.
Let's give'm a few more minutes.
MAX
FRIDAY

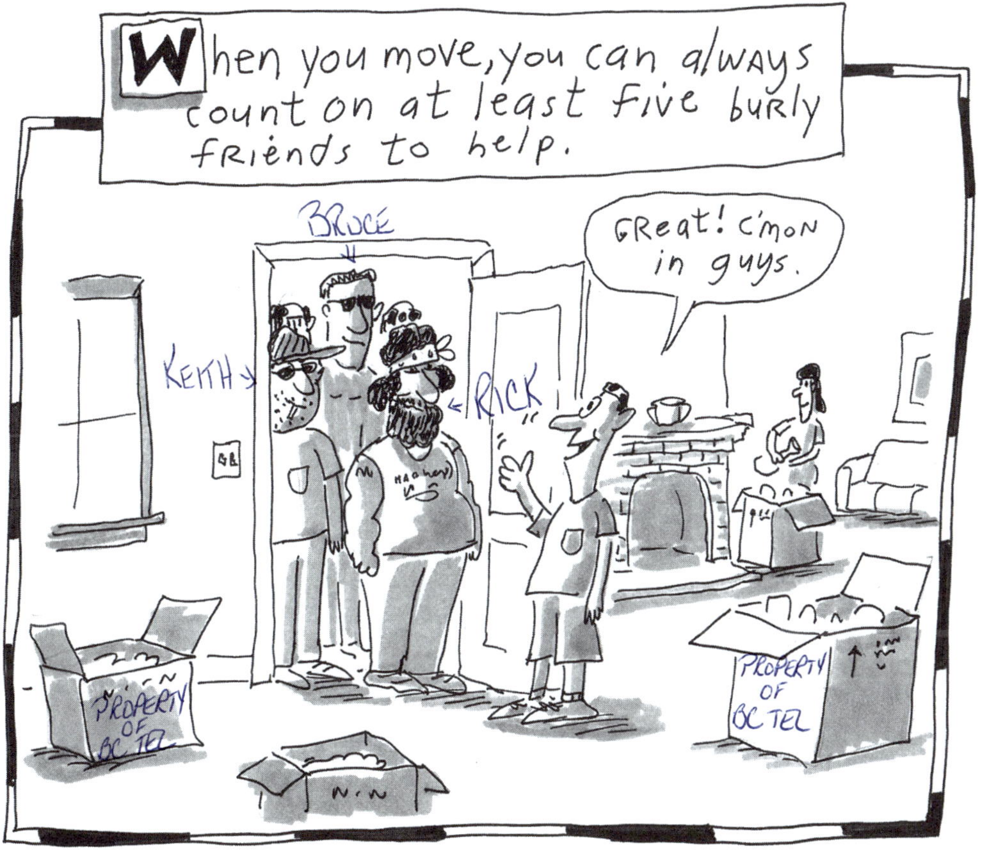
When you move, you can always count on at least five burly friends to help.
BRUCE
KEITH
RICK
GREat! c'mon in guys.
PROPERTY OF BC TEL
PROPERTY OF BC TEL

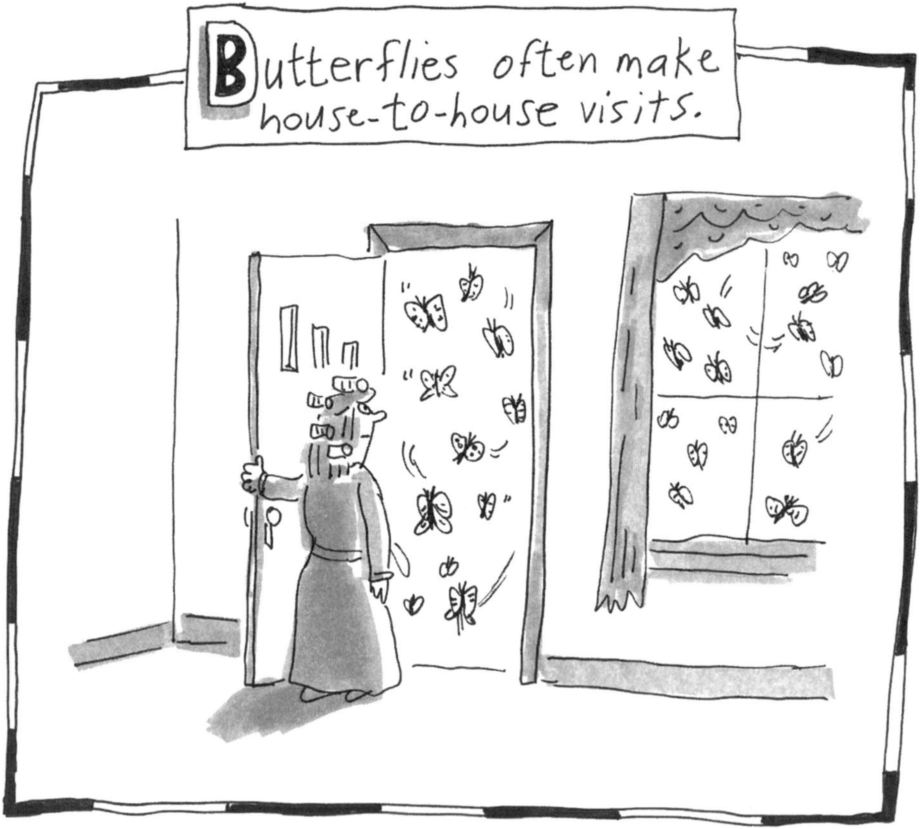
Butterflies often make house-to-house visits.

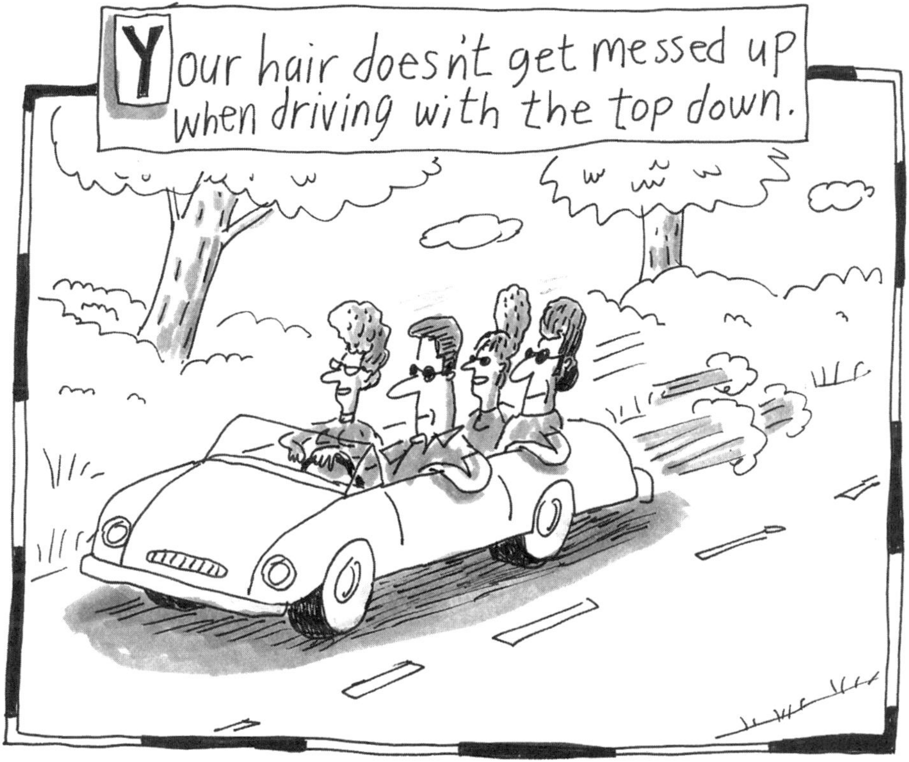
Your hair doesn't get messed up when driving with the top down.

95

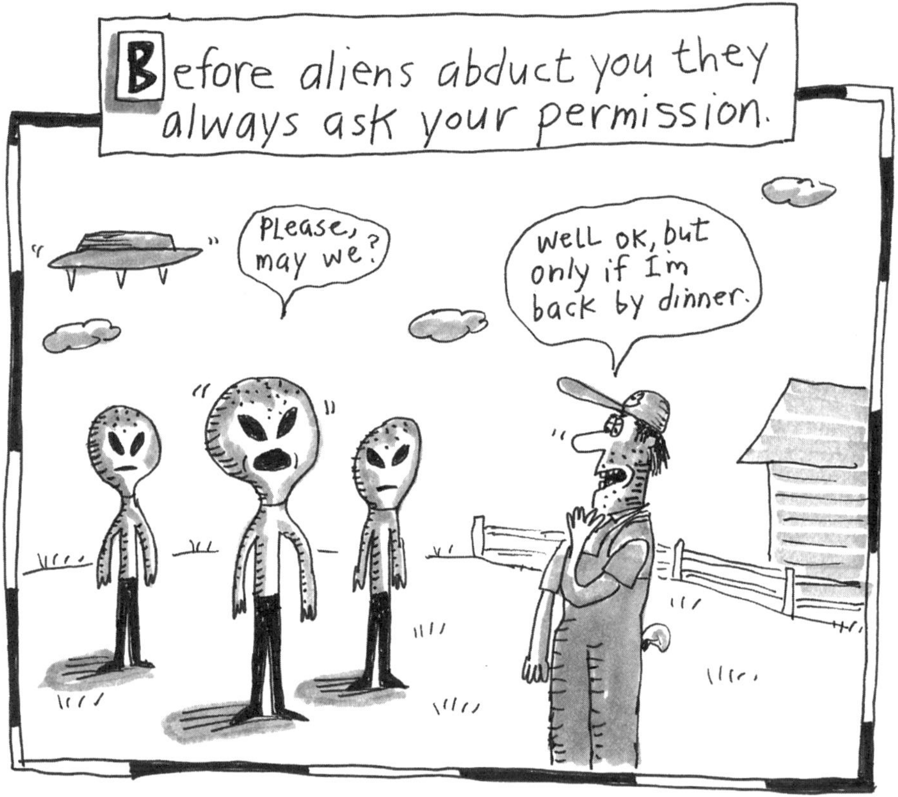
Before aliens abduct you they always ask your permission.
Please, may we?
Well OK, but only if I'm back by dinner.

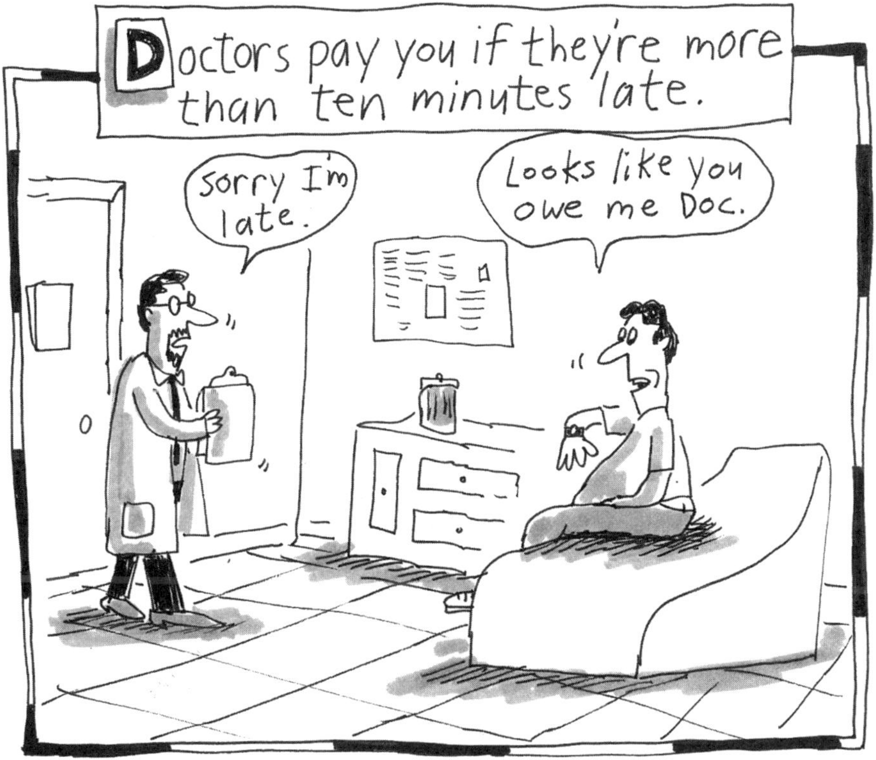
Doctors pay you if they're more than ten minutes late.
Sorry I'm late.
Looks like you owe me Doc.

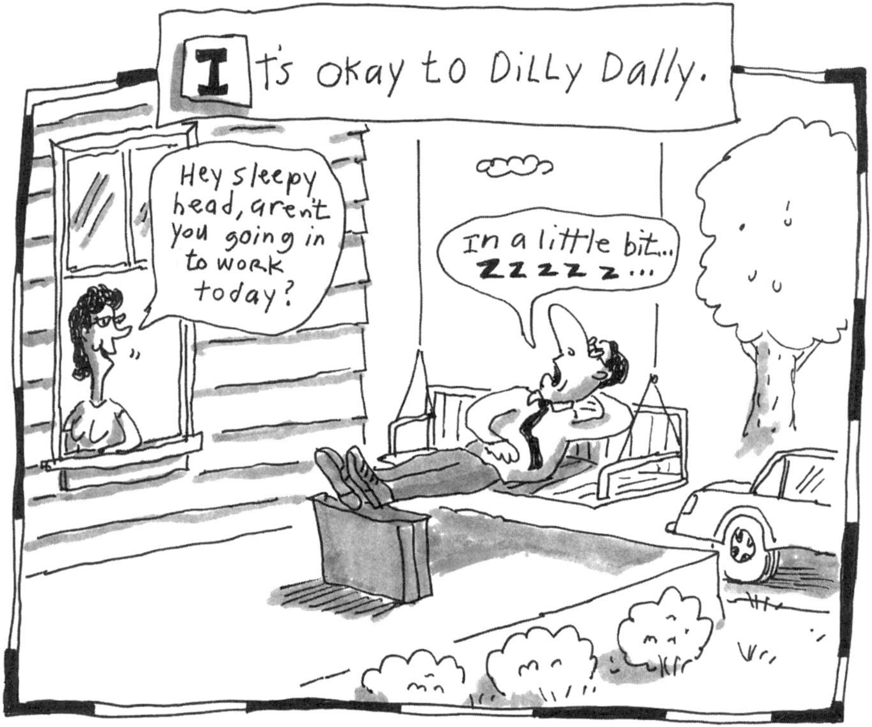
It's okay to Dilly Dally.
Hey sleepy head, aren't you going in to work today?
In a little bit... ZZZZZ...

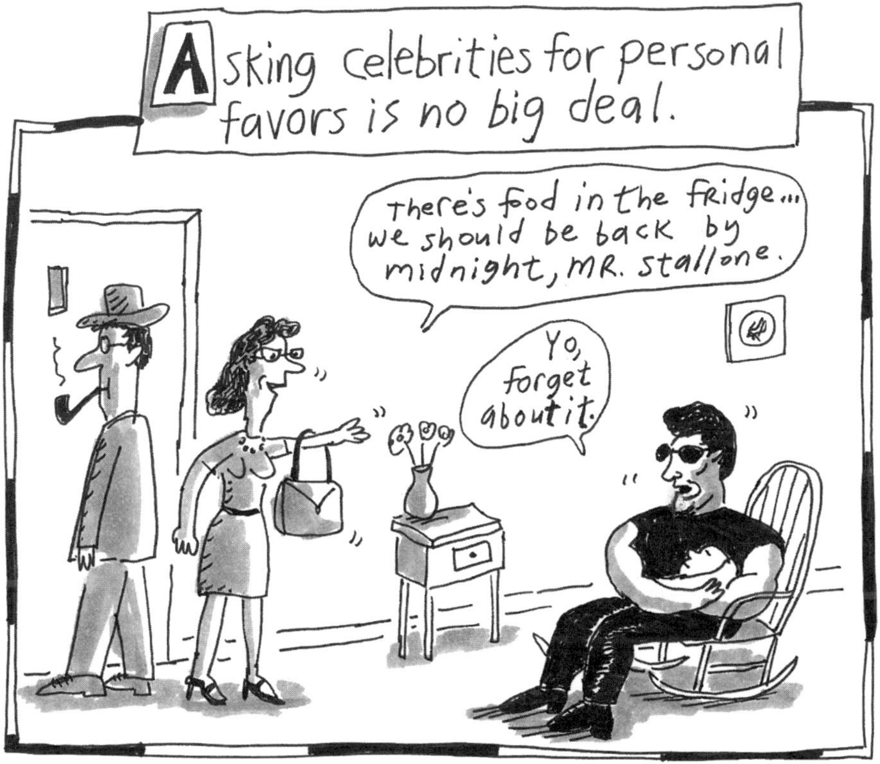
Asking celebrities for personal favors is no big deal.
There's food in the fridge... we should be back by midnight, MR. stallone.
Yo, forget about it.

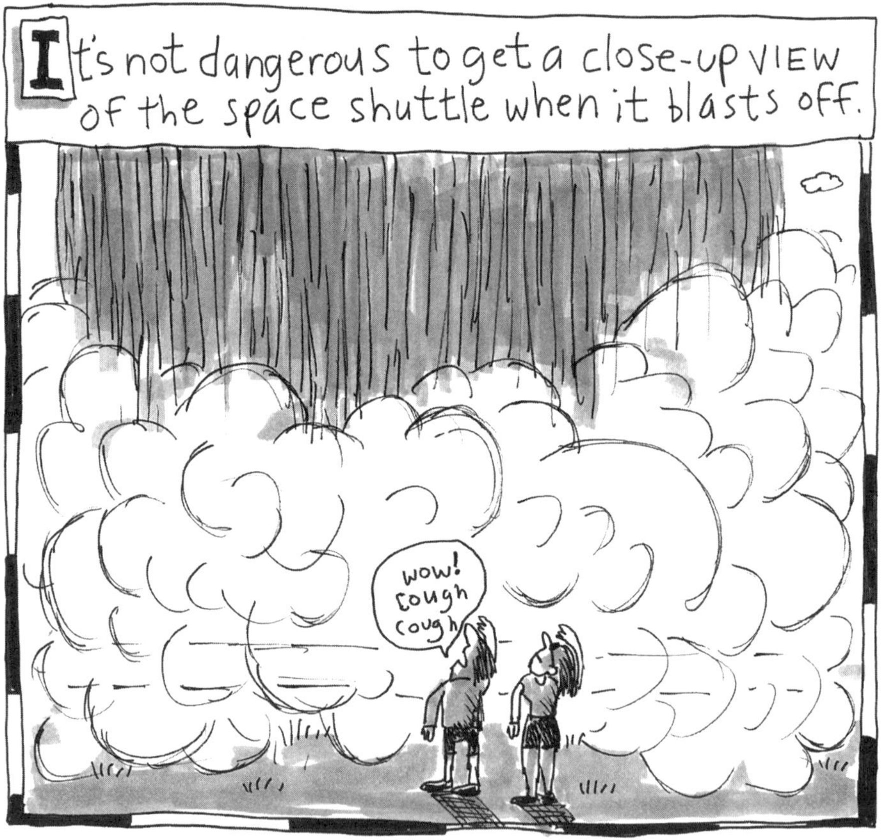
It's not dangerous to get a close-up VIEW of the space shuttle when it blasts off.
wow! cough cough

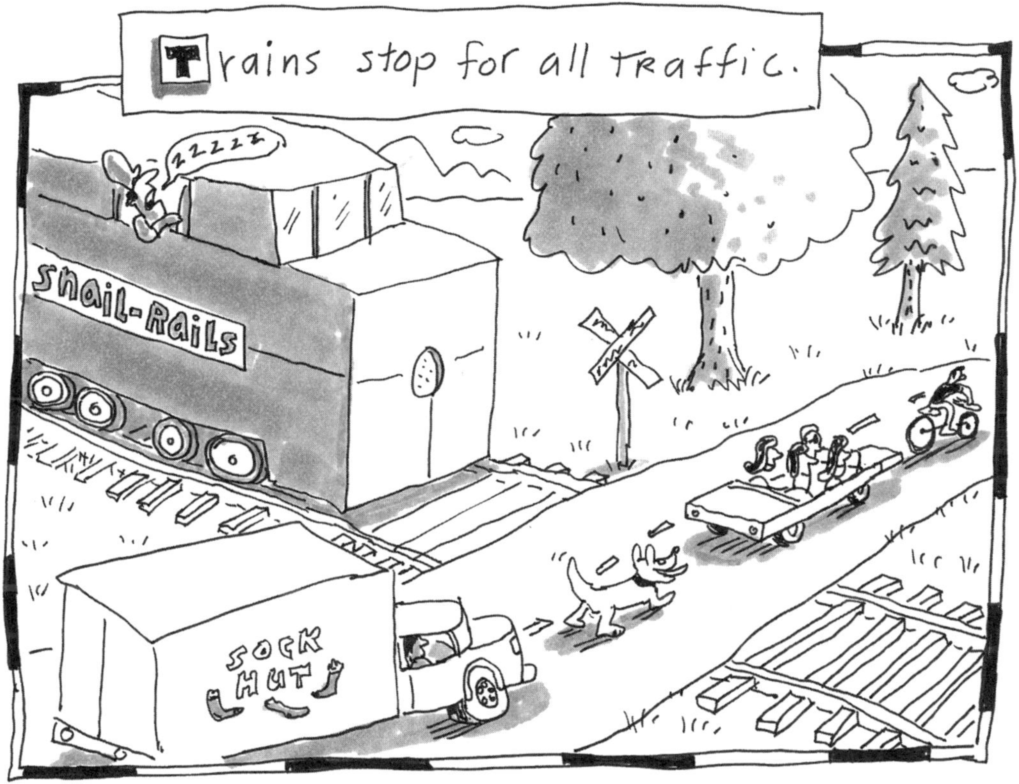
Trains stop for all traffic.
ZZZZZ
SNAIL-RAILS
SOCK HUT

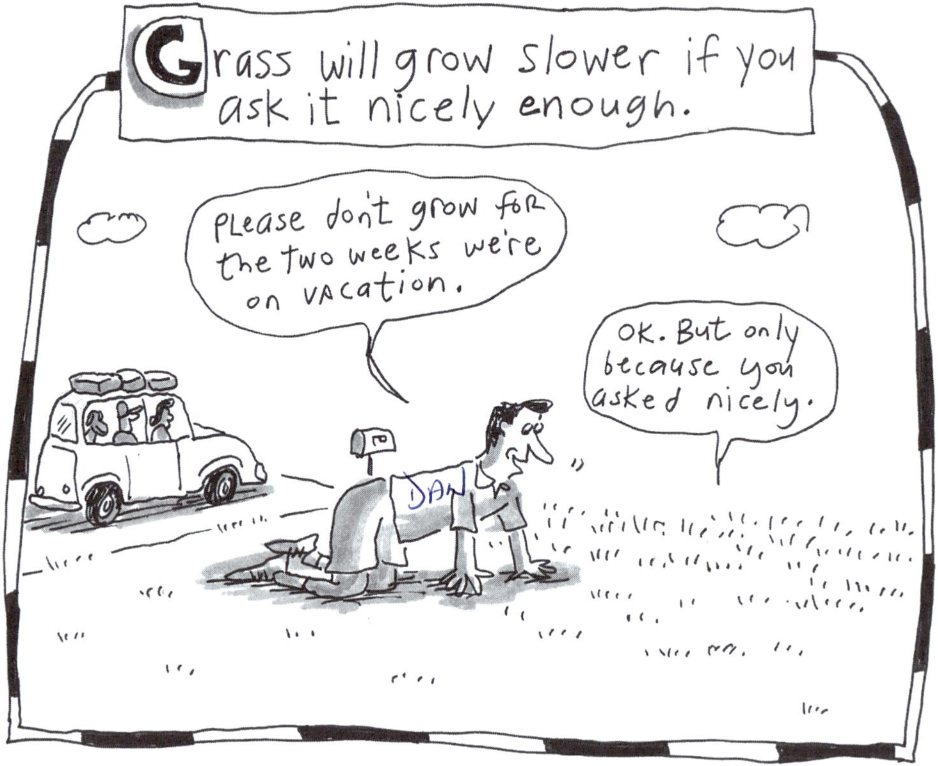
Grass will grow slower if you ask it nicely enough.
Please don't grow for the two weeks we're on vacation.
OK. But only because you asked nicely.
DAN

102

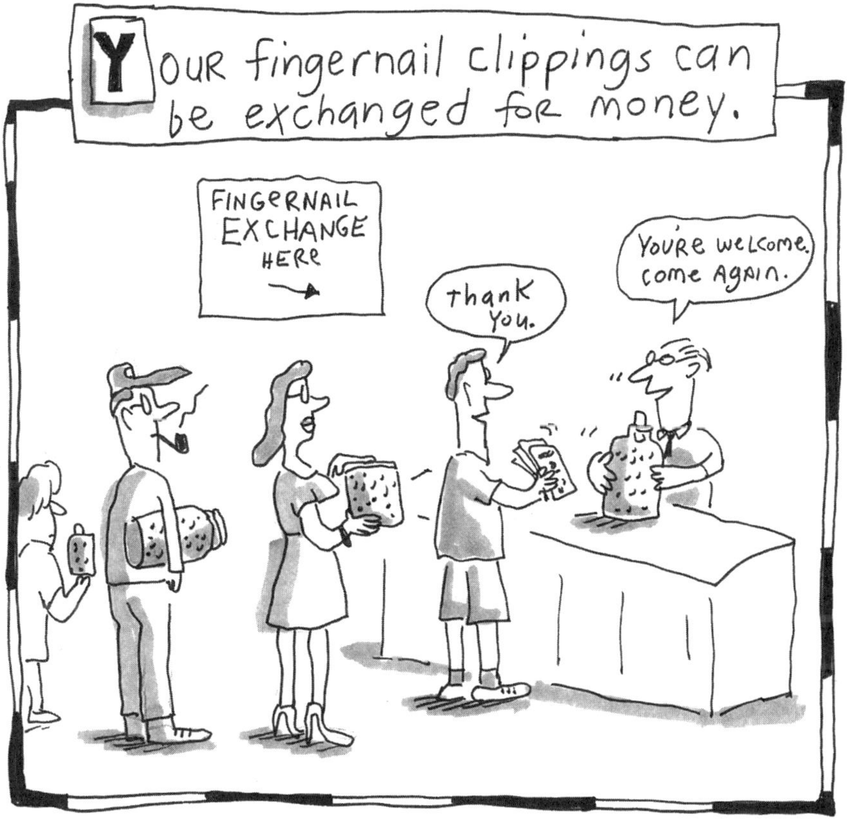
Your fingernail clippings can be exchanged for money.
FINGERNAIL EXCHANGE HERE
Thank you.
You're welcome. come AGAIN.

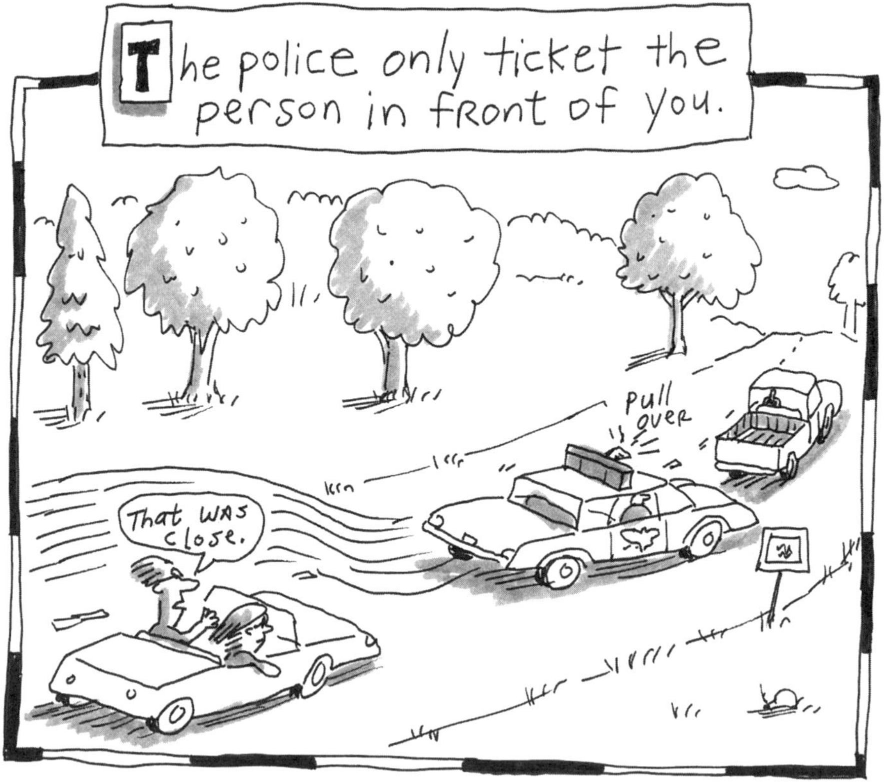
The police only ticket the person in front of you.
Pull over
That WAS close.

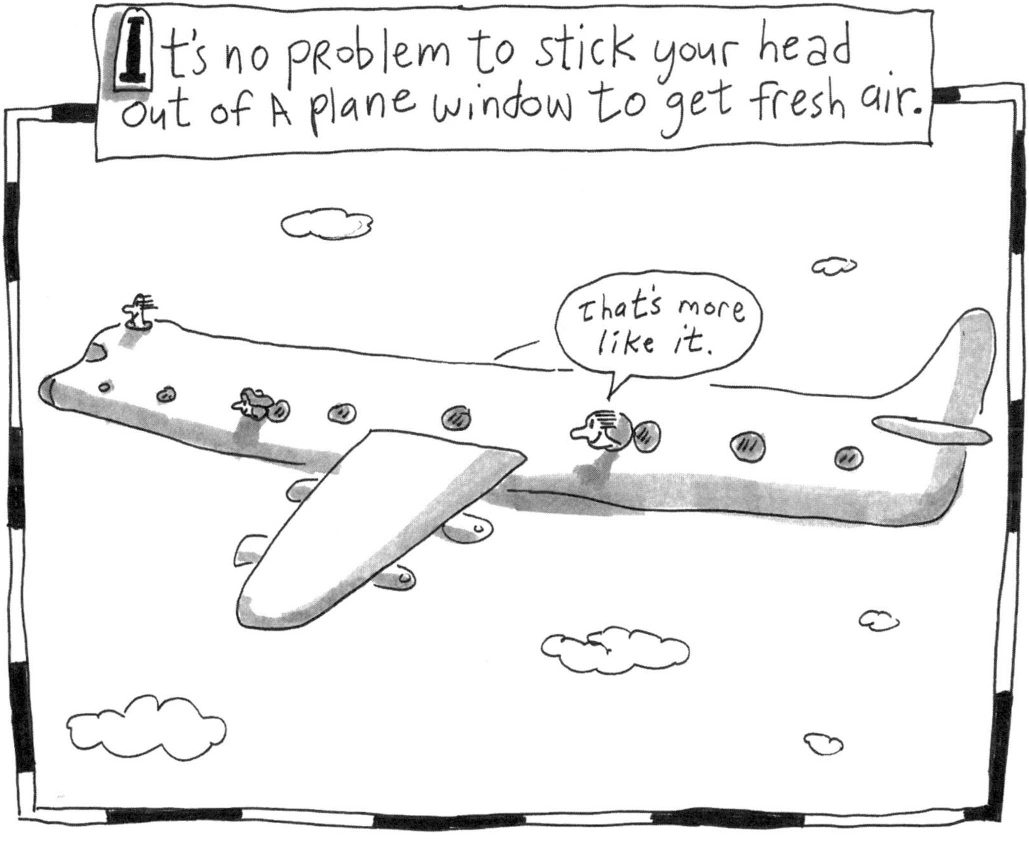
It's no problem to stick your head out of A plane window to get fresh air.
That's more like it.

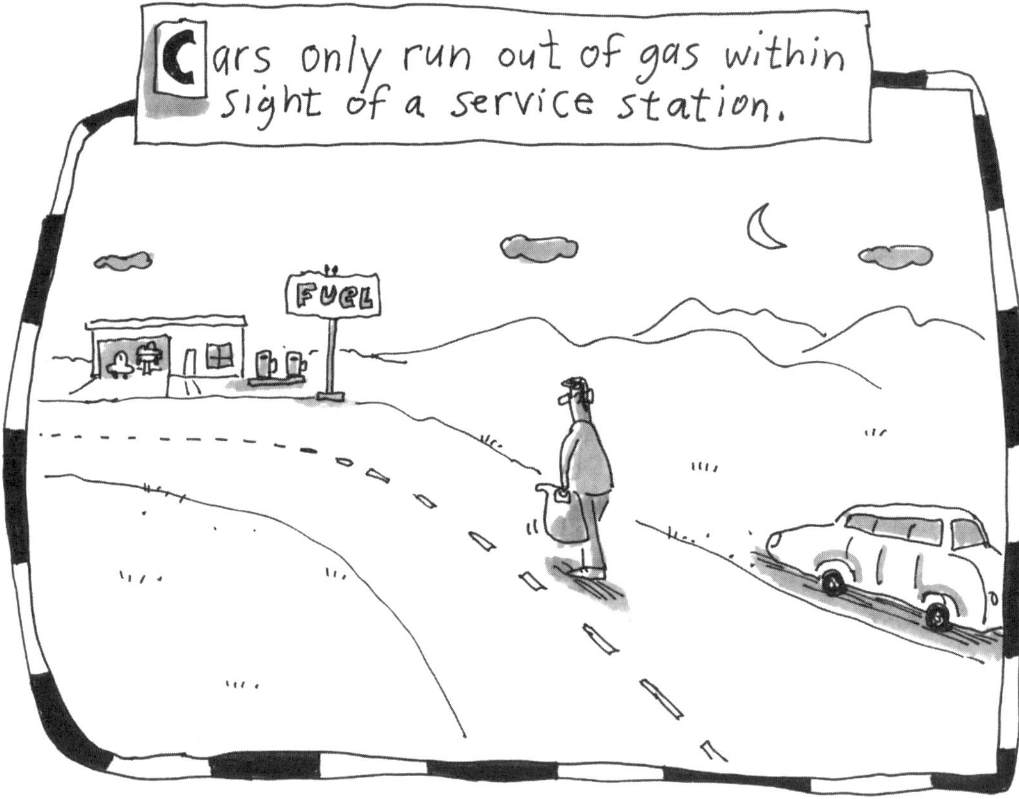
Cars only run out of gas within sight of a service station.
FUEL